STONE OF SECRETS
THE TRUE STORY OF THE PHILOSOPHER'S STONE

RICCO PIERRE

HRMTC ALKMY PUBLISHING

"I am I
Therefore, I am Self
Therefore, I am All Things but No Thing
But most importantly
I am"
— Ricco Pierre

Engravings from J.D. Mylius' *Anatomia Auri*, 1628.

STONE OF SECRETS

The True Story of the
Philosopher's Stone

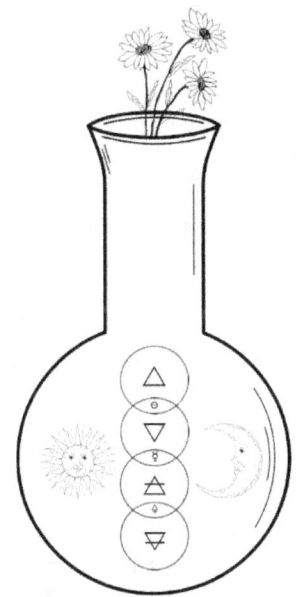

BY RICCO PIERRE

Title: *Stone of Secrets: The True Story of the Philosopher's Stone*

Author: Ricco Pierre

Publisher: HRMTC ALKMY Publishing, LLC

Published by:

HRMTC ALKMY Publishing, LLC

924 N Magnolia Ave

Ste 202 Unit 5073

Orlando, FL 32803

USA

ISBN: 979-8-9912723-7-7

Library of Congress Control Number: 2024916182

First Edition: 2024

Cover Design: Ricco Pierre

Printed in USA

For more information, visit hrmtcalkmy.com

TABLE OF CONTENTS

PREFACE

The Philosopher's Stone has long symbolized ultimate achievement and mystical transformation. To some, it represents the magnum opus of alchemy, the pinnacle of human endeavor in pursuing knowledge and mastery over nature. To others, it is the fabled fountain of youth, promising eternal life and health. For many, it is the legendary substance that can turn lead into gold, embodying the promise of infinite wealth and prosperity. This book embarks on a journey to explore the multifaceted history and enduring allure of the Philosopher's Stone, unraveling its mysteries and delving into its profound significance.

The purpose of this book is not to provide an exhaustive account of the history of alchemy but rather to focus on the key moments and figures that shaped our contemporary understanding of the Philosopher's Stone. My motivation for writing this book stems from my journey searching for the wisdom the Stone embodies and I have sought to distill alchemy's vast teachings and traditions into a concise, modern, and accessible format. I want to entertain readers and take them on a captivating journey, illuminating what it has been like for seekers throughout history to pursue the sacred Stone of the Philosopher.

This book covers the essential elements of alchemical history delving into ancient beginnings, the Islamic Golden Age, medieval European alchemy, the Renaissance and Enlightenment periods, and modern interpretations. While it does not provide a comprehensive history of alchemy, it focuses on the critical points that underscore the enduring fascination with the Philosopher's Stone.

This book is intended for the uninitiated followers of the occult and esoteric arts and the truth seekers searching for more light. It is designed to guide those who feel halted in their journey, offering insights and inspiration to continue their pursuit. Additionally, it serves as an introduction for those just beginning their exploration of alchemy, providing a clear starting point and an engaging overview of the path ahead.

The book is organized into ten chapters, each building upon the last to create a coherent narrative of the Philosopher's Stone:

1. **Ancient Beginnings**: Exploring early alchemical practices in Egypt and Greece.
2. **Islamic Golden Age**: Contributions of Islamic alchemists and the integration of ancient knowledge.
3. **Medieval European Alchemy**: Key figures and the pursuit of the Philosopher's Stone in medieval Europe.

4. **Renaissance and Enlightenment**: Revival of alchemical interests and the transition to spiritual alchemy.
5. **Modern Interpretations**: The Philosopher's Stone in literature, culture, and contemporary practices.
6. **Scientific Perspectives**: The development of modern chemistry and the legacy of alchemy.
7. **Personal Transformations and Alchemical Symbolism**: The symbolic journey of personal growth and transformation.
8. **Alchemists Who May Have Succeeded**: Profiles of legendary alchemists associated with the Philosopher's Stone.
9. **End Of The Journey:** Summary of the Historical Journey and Modern Interpretations
10. **Appendices**
    - **The Emerald Tablet of Hermes**: An analysis of its verses and their correlation with the Philosopher's Stone.
    - **A glossary** of alchemical terms, a timeline of critical events, and recommended reading and resources.

As you embark on this journey through the history and mystery of the Philosopher's Stone, I encourage you to engage deeply with the material, allowing it to inspire your quest for knowledge and transformation. Whether you are a seasoned seeker or a curious newcomer, this book will serve as a guide and a companion, illuminating the path to Enlightenment and the alchemical secrets that have captivated humanity for centuries.

PREFACE

May you find the wisdom and the wonder that you seek.

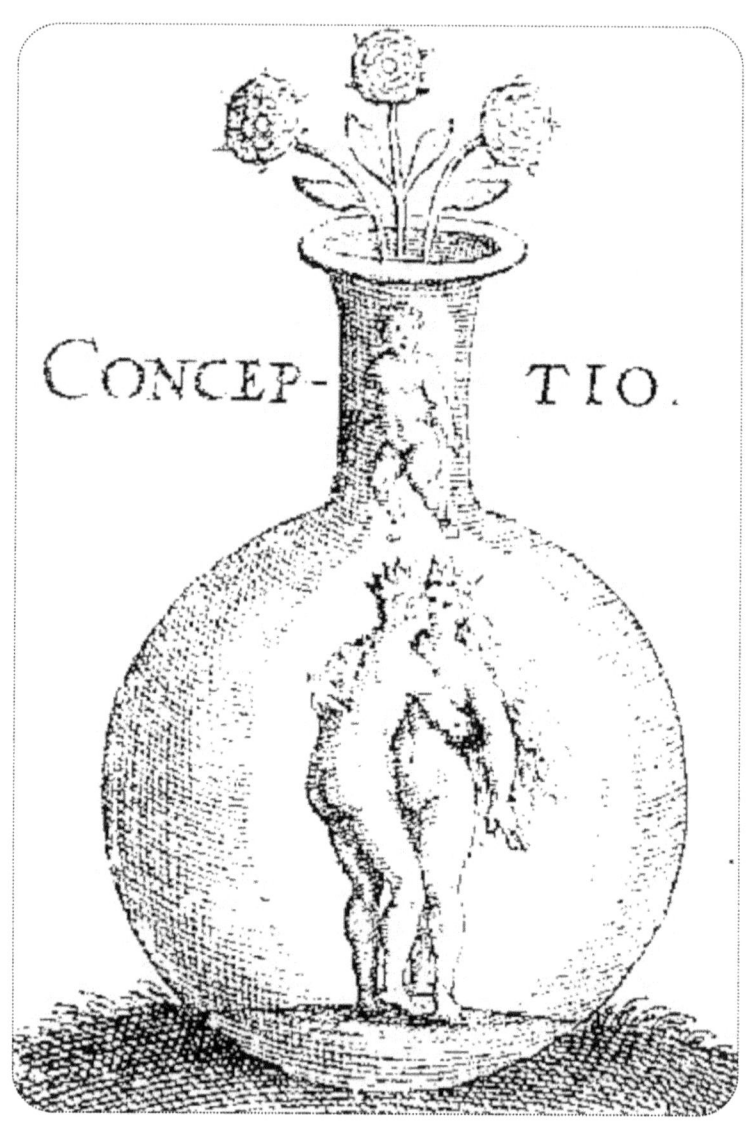

Engravings from J.D. Mylius' *Anatomia Auri*, 1628.

INTRODUCTION

The Philosopher's Stone is one of the most enduring and enigmatic symbols in the history of human thought. Often depicted as the ultimate goal of alchemy, this mythical substance was believed to possess the ability to transform base metals into gold and grant eternal life. For centuries, the quest for the Philosopher's Stone has captured the imaginations of alchemists, scholars, and adventurers, inspiring countless legends, myths, and works of art.

From the ancient temples of Egypt and the scholarly schools of Greece to the bustling streets of medieval Europe and the grand courts of the Renaissance, the Philosopher's Stone symbolizes the human desire to transcend the ordinary and achieve the extraordinary. It represents the intersection of science and mysticism, the tangible and the intangible, the earthly and the divine. The story of the Philosopher's Stone is not just a tale of magical transformations but also a profound journey into the human spirit's quest for knowledge, perfection, and Enlightenment.

In this book we unravel the complex tapestry of history,

mythology, and science surrounding the Philosopher's Stone. We will also explore the modern interpretations and symbolic meanings of the Philosopher's Stone, examining how this ancient concept continues to influence contemporary literature, popular culture, and spiritual practices. From the scientific debunking of alchemical transmutation to the philosophical reflections on the pursuit of Enlightenment, we will consider the enduring legacy of the Philosopher's Stone in today's world.

By the end of this book, you will have gained a comprehensive understanding of the Philosopher's Stone, not just as a historical and mythical object but as a symbol of humanity's relentless pursuit of transformation and transcendence. Whether you are a scholar, a seeker, or simply a curious reader, the story of the Philosopher's Stone offers a rich and fascinating window into the depths of human creativity, ambition, and imagination.

Welcome to a journey through time, myth, and science —searching for the Philosopher's Stone.

Engravings from J.D. Mylius' *Anatomia Auri*, 1628.

CHAPTER I

ANCIENT BEGINNINGS

EARLY ALCHEMICAL PRACTICES IN ANCIENT EGYPT AND GREECE

Alchemy, often regarded as the precursor to modern chemistry, originates in the ancient civilizations of Egypt and Greece. These early societies harbored a profound fascination with the natural world's mysteries and sought to understand and manipulate the elements that surrounded them. As it emerged, Alchemy developed into a blend of philosophy, mysticism, and proto-scientific inquiry aimed at uncovering the hidden properties of matter and achieving ultimate transformation.

ANCIENT EGYPT

In Ancient Egypt, alchemy was closely intertwined with religious and spiritual beliefs. The Egyptians viewed the natural world as a reflection of the divine, and their alchemical practices were deeply rooted in their mythology and cosmology. The god Thoth, often depicted as a man with the head of an ibis, was revered as the patron deity of alchemy, writing, and wisdom. Thoth was believed to possess the secrets of the heavens and the earth, including the power to transform matter through manipulating the core elements of Fire, Air, Earth, Water, and Aether (Spirit).

One of the most significant contributions the Egyptians made to alchemical thought was the concept of "khemia," which referred to the art of transmuting substances. This term later evolved into "alchemy." The Egyptians practiced various metallurgical techniques, such as alloying and purification, which laid the groundwork for later alchemical endeavors. Their expertise in working with metals like gold and copper was highly advanced, and they believed that these processes mirrored the natural transformations occurring in the cosmos.

ANCIENT GREEKS

The ancient Greeks, influenced by Egyptian knowledge, further developed alchemical ideas. Greek philosophers such as Empedocles, Plato, and Aristotle contributed to the conceptual framework that would shape alchemical thought for centuries. Empedocles proposed the existence of four fundamental elements—Earth, Water, Air, and Fire—that combined to form all matter. This idea was later elaborated by Aristotle, who introduced the concept of "prima materia," or the primary matter from which all substances are derived.

The Greeks also contributed to the mystical and symbolic aspects of alchemy. The notion of chrysopoeia, or the transmutation of base metals into gold, became a central theme in Greek alchemical thought. This concept was not merely a pursuit of material wealth but also a metaphor for spiritual purification and Enlightenment. The transformation of lead into gold symbolized the refinement of the soul and the attainment of divine wisdom.

The early alchemists believed that by understanding and mastering the processes of nature, they could accelerate and perfect the natural transformations that occurred over time. This belief was encapsulated in the concept of the Philosopher's Stone, a substance believed to possess the power to transmute base metals into gold and grant eternal life. The search for the Philosopher's Stone became a central pursuit in alchemical traditions, symbolizing the quest for ultimate knowledge and Enlightenment.

THE CONCEPT OF CHRYSOPOEIA AND EARLY METALLURGICAL PRACTICES

Chrysopoeia, derived from the Greek words "chrysos" (gold) and "poiein" (to make), epitomized the alchemist's dream of achieving perfection. In ancient alchemy, gold was considered the most noble and incorruptible metal, representing the pinnacle of material and spiritual purity. The process of chrysopoeia was seen as a sacred quest, requiring technical skill and moral and spiritual integrity.

Early metallurgical practices in Egypt and Greece provided the foundation for the pursuit of chrysopoeia. The Egyptians were skilled metallurgists known for their ability to extract and refine gold. They developed techniques such as smelting, alloying, and gilding, which allowed them to manipulate metals in sophisticated ways. These techniques were practical and symbolic, reflecting the Egyptians' belief in the transformative power of the divine.

In Greece, metallurgical knowledge was further advanced through the work of philosophers and artisans. Greek metallurgists employed techniques such as cupellation, a process for refining gold and silver, which involved separating precious metals from impurities using high temperatures.

INFLUENCE OF HERMETIC TEXTS

The influence of Hermetic texts on alchemical practices in Ancient Egypt and Greece cannot be overstated. Hermeticism, a philosophical and spiritual tradition attributed to the legendary figure Hermes Trismegistus, played a crucial role in shaping alchemical thought. Hermes Trismegistus, often identified with the Egyptian god Thoth and the Greek god Hermes, was revered as a master of alchemy, astrology, and magic.

The Hermetic texts, also known as the Corpus Hermeticum, are a collection of writings encompassing a wide range of esoteric subjects, including alchemy. These texts emphasize the interconnectedness of the material and spiritual realms, teaching that the microcosm (the individual) reflects the macrocosm (the universe).

This principle, encapsulated in the famous Hermetic maxim "As above, so below," became a cornerstone of alchemical philosophy. One of the most influential Hermetic texts is the "Emerald Tablet"(see appendices) a cryptic and concise work that outlines the principles of alchemy. The "Emerald Tablet" is attributed to Hermes Trismegistus and is often considered the foundational text of Western alchemy. Its opening lines, "That which is below is like that which is above, and that which is above is like that which is below," encapsulate the essence of Hermetic alchemy—the belief in the unity and correspondence between the material and spiritual worlds.

The teachings of the Hermetic texts inspired generations of alchemists to pursue the Great Work, the alchemical quest for the Philosopher's Stone. These texts provided practical instructions for alchemical operations and a philosophical framework that guided the alchemists' spiritual and intellectual endeavors. The Hermetic tradition emphasized the importance of inner transformation and the alignment of the alchemist's soul with the divine order of the cosmos.

As we journey through the history of the Philosopher's Stone, we will see how Ancient Egypt and Greece's early practices and philosophies laid the foundation for the following alchemical traditions. The legacy of these ancient civilizations continues to resonate in the alchemical texts, symbols, and practices passed down through the ages, shaping our understanding of the transformative power of alchemy.

In the next chapter, we will explore the contributions of Islamic alchemists during the Golden Age of Islam. These scholars built upon the knowledge of their predecessors, refining and expanding the practice of alchemy in ways that would profoundly influence medieval European alchemists and beyond.

STONE OF SECRETS

COLOR COELESTINUS

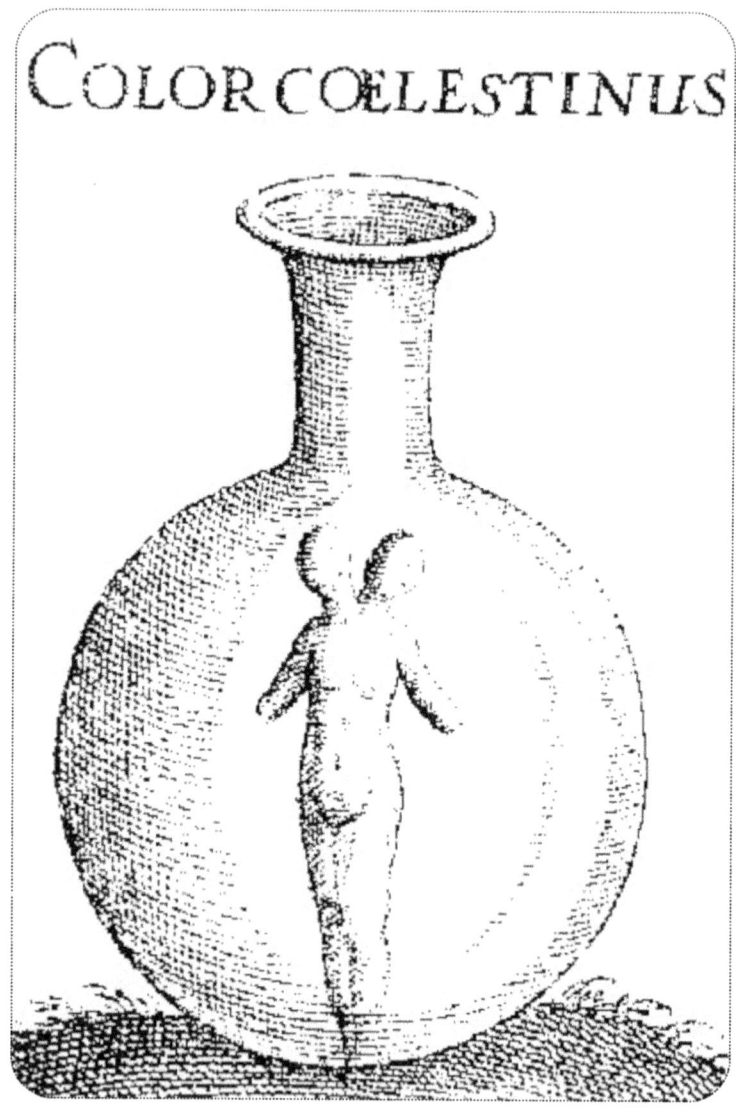

Engravings from J.D. Mylius' *Anatomia Auri*, 1628.

CHAPTER 2
ISLAMIC GOLDEN AGE

CONTRIBUTION OF ISLAMIC ALCHEMISTS

The Islamic Golden Age, from the 8th to the 14th century, was a period of remarkable intellectual and scientific achievement. During this time, the Islamic world became a center of learning and innovation, significantly contributing to the development of alchemy. Islamic alchemists not only preserved the knowledge of Ancient Egypt and Greece but also expanded and refined alchemical theories and practices.

One of the most influential figures in Islamic alchemy is Jabir ibn Hayyan, known in the West as Geber. Often regarded as the "father of chemistry," Jabir's contributions to alchemy were profound and far-reaching. He authored numerous texts that systematized alchemical knowledge and introduced new concepts and techniques. His works, such as the "Book of Seventy," laid the groundwork for later alchemical practices in the Islamic world and medieval Europe.

Jabir ibn Hayyan's approach to alchemy was meticulous and methodical. He emphasized the importance of experimentation and observation, advocating for a scientific approach to alchemical studies. Jabir introduced the concept of "al-kimiya," an evolution of the earlier Egyptian term "khemia." "Al-kimiya" included the practical techniques of metallurgy and chemistry inherited from the Egyptians and incorporated a philosophical and spiritual dimension. This perspective embraced transforming the alchemist's soul alongside physical substances. During his work, he developed processes such as distillation, crystallization, and sublimation, which became fundamental techniques in alchemy and modern chemistry.

Another notable Islamic alchemist is Al-Razi, known in the West as Rhazes. Physician and scholar, Al-Razi made significant contributions to both medicine and alchemy. His book "Kitab al-Asrar" (The Book of Secrets) detailed various chemical substances, their properties, and practical alchemical procedures. Al-Razi's work on classifying substances and understanding chemical reactions laid the foundation for future advancements in the field.

DEVELOPMENT OF ALCHEMICAL THEORIES AND PRACTICES

Islamic alchemists played a crucial role in advancing alchemical theories and practices. They built upon the knowledge inherited from ancient civilizations, integrating it with their own observations and experiments. One of the key developments during this period was the concept of the "Elixir" or "al-iksir," a substance believed to have the power to transmute base metals into gold and grant immortality.

The pursuit of the Elixir was central to Islamic alchemy and was seen as a physical and spiritual quest. Alchemists believed that by perfecting their understanding of the natural world and mastering the transformation of substances, they could attain both material wealth and spiritual Enlightenment. This dual focus on alchemy's material and spiritual aspects mirrored the Hermetic principle of the unity between the microcosm and the macrocosm.

Islamic alchemists also made significant strides in metallurgy. They developed techniques for refining metals and creating alloys essential for various practical applications. For example, the process of calcination, which involves heating a substance to a high temperature to remove impurities, was refined by Islamic alchemists and became a standard practice in metallurgy.

Another significant development was the use of laboratory equipment and the establishment of systematic procedures for conducting experiments. Islamic alchemists designed and utilized apparatus such as alembics, retorts, and crucibles to perform complex chemical reactions precisely. These innovations laid the groundwork for the modern scientific laboratory and the experimental methods used in contemporary chemistry.

INTEGRATION OF GREEK AND EGYPTIAN KNOWLEDGE

One of the defining features of Islamic alchemy was its ability to integrate and expand upon the knowledge of Ancient Greece and Egypt. Islamic scholars had access to a wealth of texts and manuscripts from these ancient civilizations, which they translated, studied, and built upon. The translation movement, centered in the House of Wisdom in Baghdad, played a pivotal role in preserving and disseminating this knowledge.

Greek philosophical and scientific texts, including the works of Aristotle, Plato, and Ptolemy, were translated into Arabic and became foundational texts for Islamic scholars. The teachings of these Greek philosophers, particularly Aristotle's theories on matter and form, heavily influenced Islamic alchemical thought. Islamic alchemists synthesized these ideas with their observations and experiments, creating a unique and sophisticated body of alchemical knowledge.

The influence of Hermetic texts also played a significant role in Islamic alchemy. The Hermetic tradition resonated deeply with Islamic alchemists, emphasizing the unity of the material and spiritual worlds. They adopted and adapted Hermetic principles, incorporating them into their own alchemical practices and writings.

One of the key figures in integrating Greek and Egyptian knowledge into Islamic alchemy was Al-Kindi, a philosopher and polymath. Al-Kindi's work on the philosophy of science and his efforts to reconcile Greek philosophical concepts with Islamic theology profoundly impacted the development of alchemical thought. His writings on the properties of substances and the nature of chemical reactions influenced subsequent generations of alchemists.

Integrating Greek and Egyptian knowledge into Islamic alchemy was more than merely a passive process of translation and preservation. Islamic alchemists actively engaged with these ancient texts, critically analyzing and expanding upon them. They introduced new concepts, refined existing theories, and developed innovative techniques, creating a vibrant and dynamic tradition of alchemical practice. Incorporating Ancient wisdom into Islamic alchemy created a rich and sophisticated tradition that would profoundly influence medieval European alchemists and beyond.

As we continue our journey through the history of the Philosopher's Stone, we will explore how the knowledge and innovations of Islamic alchemists were transmitted to medieval Europe. In the next chapter, we delve into the alchemical practices of medieval Europe, examining the key figures, texts, and ideas that shaped the pursuit of the Philosopher's Stone during this period.

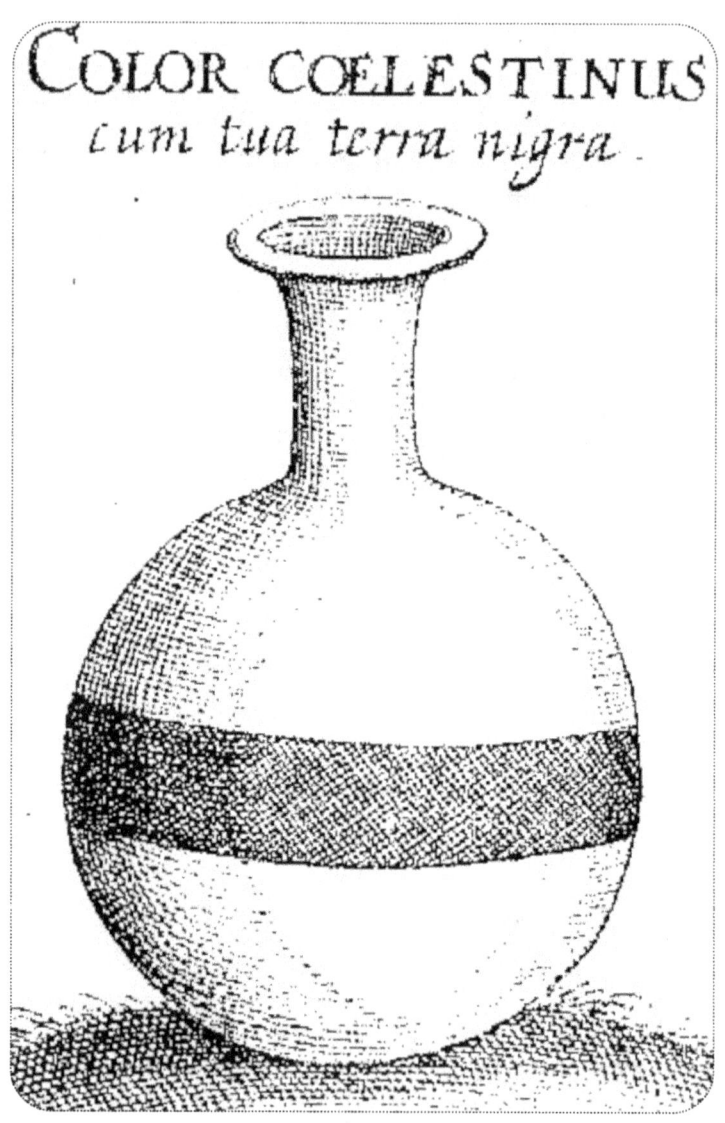

Engravings from J.D. Mylius' *Anatomia Auri,* 1628.

CHAPTER 3
MEDIEVAL EUROPEAN ALCHEMY

ALCHEMICAL PRACTICES IN MEDIEVAL EUROPE

During the medieval period, the translation of Ancient Greek and Islamic texts into Latin fueled a resurgence of interest in alchemy in Europe. This revival was part of a broader intellectual movement that sought to recover and integrate antiquity's lost knowledge. Alchemy, with its promise of material and spiritual transformations, captivated the imaginations of scholars, mystics, and even clergy members.

Medieval alchemy in Europe was characterized by its blend of practical experimentation and mystical symbolism. Alchemists were often viewed with reverence and suspicion, as their work straddled the boundary between legitimate science and esoteric practice. The goals of alchemy during this period were ambitious: the transmutation of base metals into gold, the creation of the Philosopher's Stone, and the pursuit of the Elixir of Life, believed to grant immortality and perfect health.

Alchemical practices were conducted in secret laboratories, where alchemists worked with an assortment of substances and techniques. They employed processes such as calcination, distillation, fermentation, and coagulation to manipulate materials and achieve their desired transformations. These operations were often described in symbolic and allegorical terms, with metals, plants, and animals representing different stages of the alchemical process.

One of the foundational aspects of medieval alchemy was the belief in the interconnectedness of all things. Alchemists saw the cosmos as unified, governed by hidden correspondences and analogies, echoing the Hermetic maxim "As above, so below." Alchemy, therefore, was not just a quest for material wealth but also a path to spiritual Enlightenment and self-transformation.

KEY FIGURES IN MEDIEVAL EUROPEAN ALCHEMY

Albertus Magnus

Albertus Magnus, also known as Saint Albert the Great, was a 13th-century German Dominican friar and a leading figure in medieval alchemy. He was a polymath who significantly contributed to various fields, including theology, philosophy, and natural science. Albertus Magnus is often credited with integrating Aristotelian philosophy into Christian theology, laying the groundwork for Scholasticism.

In the realm of alchemy, Albertus Magnus was known for his empirical approach to studying nature. He believed that alchemical transformations were possible by applying natural laws and that the Philosopher's Stone could be achieved by understanding and manipulating these laws.

His writings on alchemy, such as "De mineralibus" and "De alchymia," provided detailed descriptions of alchemical processes and emphasized the importance of experimentation and observation.

Albertus Magnus's contributions to alchemy influenced the field's subsequent development. His work inspired later alchemists to adopt a more systematic and scientific approach to their studies, bridging the gap between mystical speculation and empirical science.

Roger Bacon

Roger Bacon, a 13th-century English Franciscan friar, was another pivotal figure in medieval alchemy. Known as "Doctor Mirabilis" (Wonderful Teacher), Bacon was a scholar who advocated for the empirical study of nature and the use of experimentation to acquire knowledge. He was an early proponent of the scientific method and significantly contributed to various disciplines, including optics, astronomy, and mathematics.

In alchemy, Roger Bacon was particularly interested in the transmutation of metals and the quest for the Philosopher's Stone. He believed that alchemy held the key to understanding the fundamental principles of nature and that the Philosopher's Stone could unlock the secrets of immortality and eternal youth.

Bacon's alchemical writings, such as "Opus Majus" and "Speculum Alchemiae," explored alchemy's theoretical and practical aspects, emphasizing the importance of rigorous experimentation and precise observation.

Roger Bacon's work laid the foundation for the later development of experimental science. His insistence on the value of empirical evidence and his visionary ideas about the potential of alchemy to transform both matter and the human condition had a lasting impact on the history of science.

Nicolas Flamel

Nicolas Flamel, a 14th-century French scribe and manuscript seller, is one of the most famous figures associated with the legend of the Philosopher's Stone. According to popular lore, Flamel discovered the secret of the Philosopher's Stone and achieved the transmutation of base metals into gold. He was also reputed to have created the Elixir of Life, which granted him and his wife, Perenelle, extraordinary longevity. Flamel's enduring influence on the world of alchemy is profound. His life and work will be explored in greater detail in an upcoming chapter.

THE PURSUIT OF THE PHILOSOPHER'S STONE FOR IMMORTALITY AND WEALTH

The pursuit of the Philosopher's Stone during the medieval period was driven by material and spiritual motivations. Alchemists sought the Stone for its reputed ability to transmute base metals into gold and its potential to grant immortality and perfect health. The Philosopher's Stone, also known as the "Magnum Opus" or the "Great Work," was seen as the ultimate achievement of alchemical practice.

Searching for the Philosopher's Stone was a profoundly spiritual endeavor for many medieval alchemists. They believed that the process of creating the Stone mirrored the alchemist's own inner transformation. Just as base metals could be purified and perfected into gold, the alchemist's soul could be refined and elevated to spiritual Enlightenment. The alchemical process, with its purification, dissolution, and recombination stages, was viewed as a metaphor for the alchemist's journey toward self-realization and divine wisdom.

However, the material allure of the Philosopher's Stone was also a powerful motivator. The ability to transmute base metals into gold promised immense wealth and economic power. Alchemical texts often included elaborate recipes and instructions for achieving this transformation. However, these were frequently encoded in symbolic and allegorical language to protect the secrets from the uninitiated.

Another critical aspect of pursuing the Philosopher's Stone was the quest for immortality, symbolized by the Elixir of Life. Alchemists believed the Elixir, derived from the Stone, could cure all diseases, restore youth, and extend life indefinitely. This belief was rooted in the idea that the Philosopher's Stone represented the quintessence of life. This perfect and incorruptible substance could bestow health and longevity for those possessing it.

The pursuit of the Philosopher's Stone for immortality and wealth was not without its dangers. Alchemists often faced skepticism, persecution, and even accusations of heresy. The secretive nature of alchemical practices and the potential for fraud and deception made alchemy a controversial and precarious profession. Nevertheless, the allure of the Philosopher's Stone continued to inspire and drive alchemists throughout the medieval period and beyond.

Medieval European alchemy was a rich and complex

tradition, blending practical experimentation with mystical and spiritual aspirations. Key figures such as Albertus Magnus, Roger Bacon, and Nicolas Flamel were pivotal in advancing alchemical knowledge and shaping the quest for the Philosopher's Stone. Their contributions laid the foundation for later developments in alchemy. They helped bridge the gap between medieval and modern scientific thought.

As we explore the history of the Philosopher's Stone, we will see how the legacy of medieval alchemy influenced the Renaissance and Enlightenment periods, leading to new interpretations and discoveries.

In the next chapter, we will delve into the Renaissance and Enlightenment, examining the revival of alchemical interests, the influence of Hermeticism, and the transition from physical to spiritual alchemy.

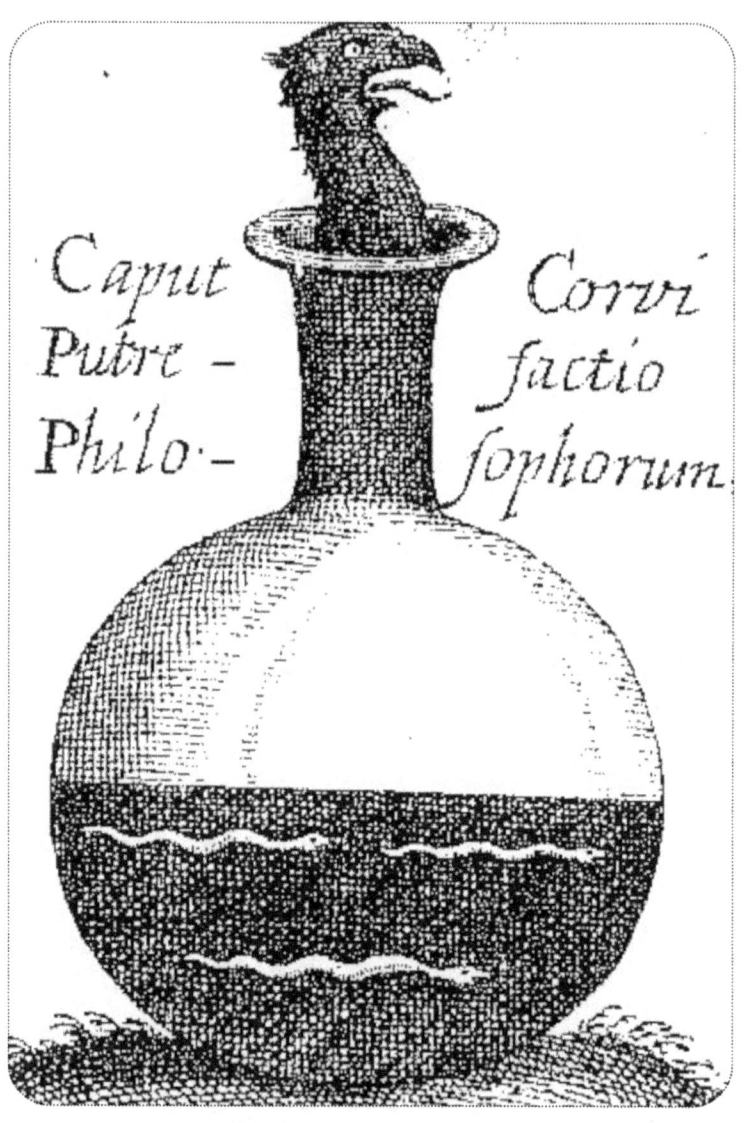

Engravings from J.D. Mylius' *Anatomia Auri*, 1628.

CHAPTER 4

RENAISSANCE AND ENLIGHTENMENT

REVIVAL OF ALCHEMICAL INTERESTS DURING THE RENAISSANCE

The Renaissance, a period of cultural rebirth and intellectual exploration spanning the 14th to the 17th century, saw a renewed interest in alchemy. This revival was fueled by the rediscovery of classical texts, the flourishing of humanist scholarship, and a growing curiosity about the natural world. With its blend of scientific inquiry and mystical philosophy, Alchemy found fertile ground in this vibrant intellectual climate.

Renaissance alchemists sought to integrate the knowledge of ancient alchemists with contemporary scientific advancements. They were inspired by the works of Ancient Greek and Roman scholars and the contributions of Islamic alchemists. Translating vital alchemical texts into Latin, including those attributed to Hermes Trismegistus, played a crucial role in this revival. These texts provided Renaissance scholars with a rich repository of alchemical knowledge, which they sought to expand and refine.

Prominent figures like Paracelsus, a Swiss physician and alchemist, exemplified the Renaissance spirit of inquiry and innovation. Paracelsus challenged the traditional medical practices of his time, advocating for a holistic approach that combined alchemical principles with practical medicine. He introduced the concept of "spagyria," the alchemical preparation of medicines, and emphasized the importance of understanding the chemical properties of substances to treat illnesses effectively.

The revival of alchemical interests during the Renaissance was also marked by the establishment of alchemical societies and the patronage of influential figures. Alchemical societies provided a forum for the exchange of ideas and collaboration among alchemists. At the same time, patrons such as emperors, kings, and nobles supported alchemical research and experimentation. These developments helped to legitimize alchemy as a respected field of study and facilitated the dissemination of alchemical knowledge.

HERMETICISM AND MYSTICAL ASPECTS OF THE PHILOSOPHER'S STONE

Hermeticism played a central role in Renaissance alchemy. The Hermetic texts, collectively known as the Corpus Hermeticum, emphasized the unity of the material and spiritual worlds and the possibility of achieving divine wisdom through studying nature. This worldview resonated deeply with Renaissance alchemists, who saw their work as a scientific and spiritual pursuit.

In the Hermetic tradition, the Philosopher's Stone was

seen as more than just a substance that could transmute base metals into gold. It was also a symbol of the perfected soul and the ultimate goal of the alchemical quest. The creation of the Philosopher's Stone was believed to require technical skill and moral and spiritual purity. Alchemists who sought the Stone were thus engaged in inner transformation, striving to purify their souls as they purified and transformed matter.

Renaissance alchemists were deeply influenced by the mystical aspects of Hermeticism. They incorporated symbols, allegories, and rituals into their work, viewing the alchemical process as a sacred journey toward self-realization and divine union. This mystical dimension of alchemy was reflected in the elaborate imagery and symbolism found in alchemical texts and artwork, which often depicted the stages of the alchemical process as a series of spiritual trials and revelations.

TRANSITION FROM PHYSICAL TO SPIRITUAL ALCHEMY

Alchemy underwent a significant transformation during the Renaissance and Enlightenment, evolving from focusing principally on physical transmutation to a more spiritual and psychological interpretation. This shift was influenced by changing philosophical perspectives, the rise of empirical science, and Hermeticism's continued influence.

One of the key figures in this transition was Heinrich Cornelius Agrippa, a Renaissance philosopher and occultist. Agrippa's "Three Books of Occult Philosophy" integrated alchemical principles with astrology, magic, and mysticism. He emphasized alchemy's spiritual and symbolic dimensions, viewing the alchemical process as a means of achieving personal and cosmic harmony. Agrippa's ideas helped to pave the way for a more introspective and spiritual approach to alchemy.

Another influential figure was John Dee, an English mathematician, astronomer, and alchemist. Dee's work was characterized by a deep interest in scientific and mystical pursuits. He sought to understand the underlying principles of the cosmos and believed that alchemy held the key to unlocking divine knowledge. Dee's collaboration with the alchemist Edward Kelley in the quest for the Philosopher's Stone and establishing communication with angelic beings exemplified the fusion of alchemy with spiritual and esoteric practices.

The transition from physical to spiritual alchemy was further advanced by the work of Jacob Boehme, a German mystic and alchemist. Boehme's writings emphasized the inner, spiritual aspect of alchemical transformation. He viewed the alchemical process as a metaphor for the soul's journey toward divine illumination and self-realization. Boehme's ideas influenced later esoteric traditions, including Rosicrucianism and Theosophy, which continued exploring alchemy's spiritual dimensions.

The Enlightenment, with its emphasis on reason, empiricism, and scientific inquiry, also played a role in the evolution of alchemy. While the rise of modern chemistry led to the decline of traditional alchemy as a scientific practice, the symbolic and spiritual aspects of alchemy persisted. Enlightenment thinkers such as Isaac Newton and Robert Boyle, who were deeply interested in alchemy, contributed to modern science's development while recognizing alchemical traditions' philosophical and spiritual insights.

The shift toward spiritual alchemy during the Renaissance and Enlightenment reflected a broader cultural and intellectual movement that sought to reconcile human existence's material and spiritual dimensions. In its evolving forms, Alchemy continued to inspire seekers of knowledge and wisdom, offering a rich symbolic framework for understanding the mysteries of nature and the human soul.

Inspired by the principles of Hermeticism, Renaissance alchemists viewed their work as both a scientific and spiritual pursuit. The creation of the Philosopher's Stone was seen as a means of achieving material transmutation and spiritual Enlightenment. As alchemy evolved during the Enlightenment, its symbolic and mystical dimensions inspired and influenced thinkers, laying the groundwork for developing modern science and esoteric traditions.

In the next chapter, we will explore the modern interpretations of the Philosopher's Stone, examining how this ancient concept continues to resonate in contemporary literature, popular culture, and spiritual practices. We will also consider the scientific perspectives on alchemy and its legacy in the development of modern chemistry and the pursuit of knowledge.

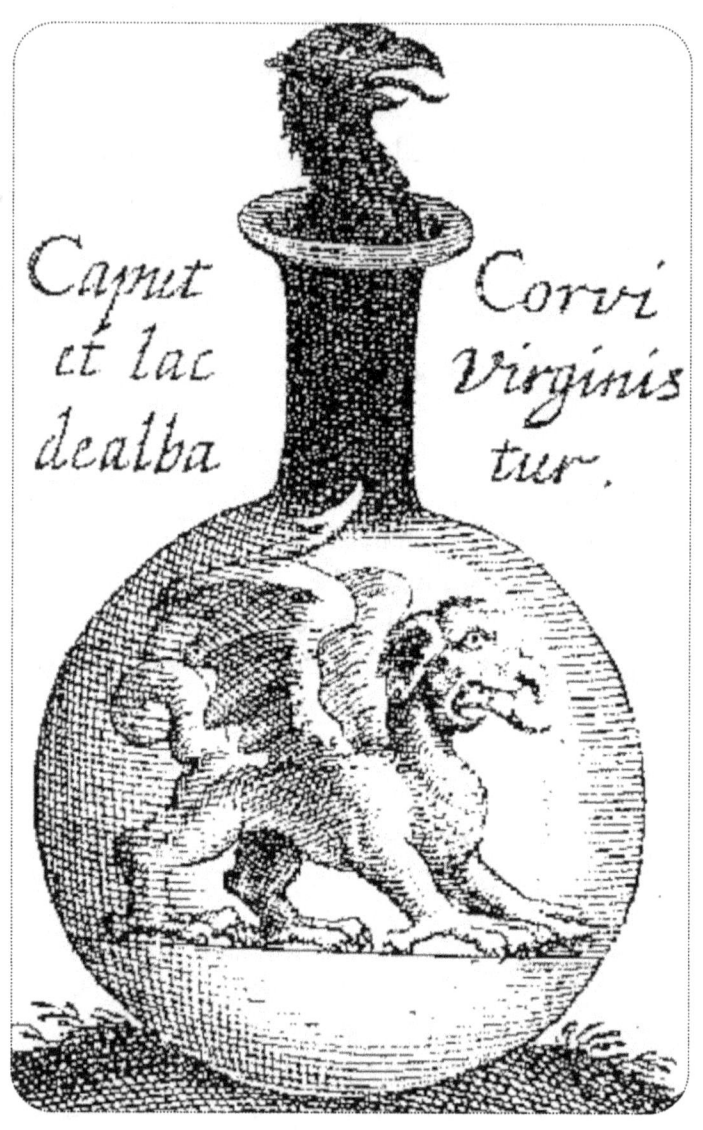

Engravings from J.D. Mylius' *Anatomia Auri,* 1628.

CHAPTER 5

MODERN INTERPRETATIONS

THE PHILOSOPHER'S STONE IN LITERATURE AND POPULAR CULTURE

The allure of the Philosopher's Stone has transcended centuries, finding new life in modern literature and popular culture. Its rich symbolism and promise of transformation have made it a compelling element in various artistic and narrative forms, and from classic literature to contemporary fiction, the Philosopher's Stone continues to captivate the imagination of audiences worldwide.

One of the most iconic modern references to the Philosopher's Stone is found in J.K. Rowling's "Harry Potter" series. In the first book, "Harry Potter and the Philosopher's Stone" (published as "Harry Potter and the Sorcerer's Stone" in the United States), the Stone is depicted as a magical object that grants immortality and turns any metal into pure gold. The story revolves around the young wizard Harry Potter's quest to prevent the dark wizard Voldemort from obtaining the

Stone. Rowling's use of the Philosopher's Stone introduces young readers to alchemical concepts while weaving them into an engaging and magical narrative.

The Philosopher's Stone also appears in other notable works of literature. In Paulo Coelho's "The Alchemist," the protagonist Santiago embarks on a journey to discover his "Personal Legend" and ultimately learns that the true Philosopher's Stone is the realization of one's own potential and destiny. Coelho's novel uses the Stone as a metaphor for personal transformation and pursuing one's true calling.

In addition to literature, the Philosopher's Stone has appeared in films, television shows, and video games. Movies like "The Seventh Seal" and "Fullmetal Alchemist" explore alchemical themes and the quest for the Stone. The Stone's portrayal in popular culture often emphasizes themes of immortality, Enlightenment, and the moral implications of seeking ultimate power.

SYMBOLISM AND METAPHORS IN MODERN TIMES

The Philosopher's Stone has evolved as a symbol to embody various metaphors in modern times. Its association with transformation, Enlightenment, and potential realization resonates with contemporary psychology, philosophy, and self-improvement themes.

The Philosopher's Stone is often used as a metaphor for personal growth and self-actualization in psychology. Carl Jung, the Swiss psychiatrist and psychoanalyst, extensively explored alchemical symbolism in his work. Jung viewed alchemy as a symbolic representation of the individuation process—the journey toward integrating different aspects of the self to achieve wholeness. For Jung, the Philosopher's

Stone represented the ultimate goal of this process: the realization of the true self.

The Stone's symbolism extends to the realm of philosophy, where it is seen as a metaphor for the pursuit of wisdom and knowledge. The alchemical process of transforming base metals into gold parallels the philosophical quest to transform ignorance into understanding and uncover the deeper truths of existence. This metaphorical use of the Philosopher's Stone underscores the idea that true Enlightenment comes from within and involves a profound inner transformation.

INFLUENCE ON CONTEMPORARY SPIRITUAL AND SELF-HELP MOVEMENTS

The legacy of the Philosopher's Stone has significant influence on contemporary spiritual and self-help movements. Its themes of transformation, Enlightenment, and integrating the material and spiritual worlds resonate deeply with modern seekers of knowledge and self-fulfillment.

In contemporary spirituality, the Philosopher's Stone is often associated with practices that aim to achieve holistic well-being and spiritual Enlightenment. Movements such as New Age spirituality, modern Hermeticism, and certain branches of Theosophy draw on alchemical symbolism to convey inner transformation and attain higher consciousness. These practices emphasize mind, body, and spirit interconnectedness, advocating for a balanced and harmonious approach to personal development.

In the self-help and personal development world, the Philosopher's Stone symbolizes the potential for self-improvement and attaining one's highest aspirations. Many contemporary self-help movements draw on alchemical metaphors to illustrate the process of personal transformation. Turning "lead" into "gold"—metaphorically transforming one's limitations and challenges into strengths and successes—is a powerful and motivating concept in the pursuit of personal growth.

Modern alchemical practices also find expression in various holistic healing modalities. Techniques such as Reiki, crystal healing, and energy work incorporate alchemical principles to promote healing and balance. Practitioners of these modalities often view the body and mind as dynamic systems that can be transformed and harmonized by applying alchemical processes.

The influence of the Philosopher's Stone extends to the world of self-help and motivational literature. Books and programs focusing on personal development frequently use alchemical metaphors to illustrate overcoming challenges and achieving one's goals. Transforming one's life through intentional actions and positive thinking is a central theme in many self-help philosophies, reflecting the alchemical principle of achieving transformation through focused effort and inner work.

The Philosopher's Stone, with its rich history and profound symbolism, continues to captivate and inspire in modern times. Its presence in literature, popular culture, psychology, and contemporary spiritual and self-help movements highlights its enduring relevance and universal appeal. As a symbol of transformation, Enlightenment, and the realization of potential, the Philosopher's Stone is a powerful metaphor for the human quest for knowledge, growth, and self-fulfillment.

In the next chapter, we explore the scientific perspectives on alchemy and its legacy in the development of modern chemistry. We will examine how the principles and practices of alchemy laid the groundwork for scientific revolution and the pursuit of empirical knowledge, bridging the gap between mystical traditions and contemporary science.

Engravings from J.D. Mylius' *Anatomia Auri*, 1628.

CHAPTER 6
SCIENTIFIC PERSPECTIVES

MODERN CHEMISTRY AND THE DEBUNKING OF ALCHEMICAL TRANSMUTATION

As the Renaissance gave way to the Enlightenment, the ensuing scientific revolution began to shift how the natural world was understood and studied. Alchemy, which had long been a blend of mysticism, philosophy, and proto-science, started to be scrutinized through the lens of empirical investigation and rational inquiry. This shift led to the development of modern chemistry, which systematically debunked many of the core tenets of alchemical transmutation.

One of the pivotal figures in this transformation was Antoine Lavoisier, often referred to as the "father of modern chemistry." In the late 18th century, Lavoisier's work in defining the principles of chemical reactions and the conservation of mass fundamentally altered the scientific landscape. He demonstrated that substances undergo chemical changes based on predictable laws and that matter cannot be created or destroyed in chemical reactions. These findings challenged the alchemical notion that base metals could be transformed into gold through mysterious and esoteric processes.

The discovery of the elements and the development of the periodic table by Dmitri Mendeleev in the 19th century further solidified the scientific understanding of matter. The periodic table categorized elements based on their atomic structure and properties, providing a clear framework that explained why the transmutation of elements, as envisioned by alchemists, was not feasible. Each element was recognized as a distinct entity with specific characteristics, debunking the alchemical idea that elements could be fundamentally transformed into one another.

Additionally, advancements in atomic theory and understanding nuclear reactions in the 20th century offered a more in-depth explanation of why alchemical transmutation was impossible with the techniques available to historical alchemists. While modern science acknowledges that nuclear reactions can change one element into another, such processes require conditions and technologies far beyond the reach of medieval and Renaissance alchemists. These scientific advancements underscored the limitations of alchemical practices while highlighting the value of empirical research and experimentation.

THE LEGACY OF ALCHEMY IN THE DEVELOPMENT OF MODERN SCIENCE

Despite the debunking of alchemical transmutation, alchemy's legacy still played a significant role in the development of modern science. Alchemists' dedication to experimentation, the development of laboratory techniques, and the quest for understanding the natural world laid essential foundations for modern chemistry and other scientific disciplines.

Alchemists were among the first to systematically experiment, meticulously recording their procedures and results. Their work with various substances and chemical processes contributed to the early development of laboratory apparatus and techniques. For example, in modern chemistry labs, distillation, filtration, and crystallization—methods perfected by alchemists—are still fundamental procedures. The alchemical laboratory, focusing on empirical observation and controlled experimentation, can be seen as a precursor to the modern scientific laboratory.

Moreover, alchemy's emphasis on understanding the properties and behaviors of substances contributed to the broader field of material science. Alchemists' explorations into metallurgy, pharmacology, and the properties of minerals and plants provided valuable knowledge that informed later scientific advancements. Their work in developing medicines and understanding the effects of various compounds on the human body laid the groundwork for modern pharmacology and medicine.

The intellectual framework of alchemy, integrating philosophy, mysticism, and science, also influenced the development of scientific thinking. Alchemists viewed the natural world as a complex, interconnected system, an idea that resonated with later scientific explorations into the relationships between different fields of study. The holistic perspective of alchemy, which sought to unify disparate elements into a cohesive understanding, is a precursor to interdisciplinary approaches in modern science.

PHILOSOPHICAL REFLECTIONS ON THE PURSUIT
OF KNOWLEDGE AND TRANSFORMATION

The philosophical dimensions of alchemy, particularly its emphasis on transformation and the quest for ultimate knowledge, continue to resonate in contemporary reflections on science and human understanding. Alchemy's metaphorical and symbolic language offers rich insights into the nature of the scientific endeavor and the human desire for transformation.

One of the enduring legacies of alchemy is its portrayal of the pursuit of knowledge as a transformative journey. Alchemists saw their work as a means to material ends and a path to spiritual and intellectual Enlightenment. This perspective aligns with the modern view of scientific inquiry as a quest for deeper understanding and the continual refinement of knowledge. The idea that the discovery process is as important as the outcomes reflects the alchemical belief in the value of the journey itself.

Alchemy's symbolic representation of transformation—turning base metals into gold—can be seen as a metaphor for the transformative power of knowledge. Just as alchemists sought to purify and perfect matter, scientists strive to refine and expand human understanding, transforming ignorance into insight. This metaphor underscores the dynamic and evolving nature of knowledge, emphasizing the ongoing process of learning and discovery.

Moreover, encapsulated in the Hermetic maxim "As above, so below," the alchemical correspondence principle highlights the interconnectedness of different knowledge domains. This principle suggests that understanding one aspect of the natural world can provide insights into other areas, encouraging a holistic and integrative approach to scientific inquiry. In modern science, this interconnectedness is reflected in interdisciplinary research, where insights from one field inform and enhance understanding in others.

Finally, alchemy's philosophical reflections remind us of the ethical dimensions of the pursuit of knowledge. Alchemists believed that achieving the Philosopher's Stone required technical skill and moral and spiritual integrity. This belief underscores the importance of ethical considerations in scientific research and the responsibility of scientists to use their knowledge for the betterment of humanity.

The transition from alchemy to modern chemistry represents a significant milestone in the history of science. Alchemy's legacy endures in the methodologies, techniques, and philosophical insights it bequeathed to modern science. The alchemical pursuit of knowledge, emphasizing transformation, interconnectedness, and ethical considerations, inspires and informs contemporary scientific inquiry.

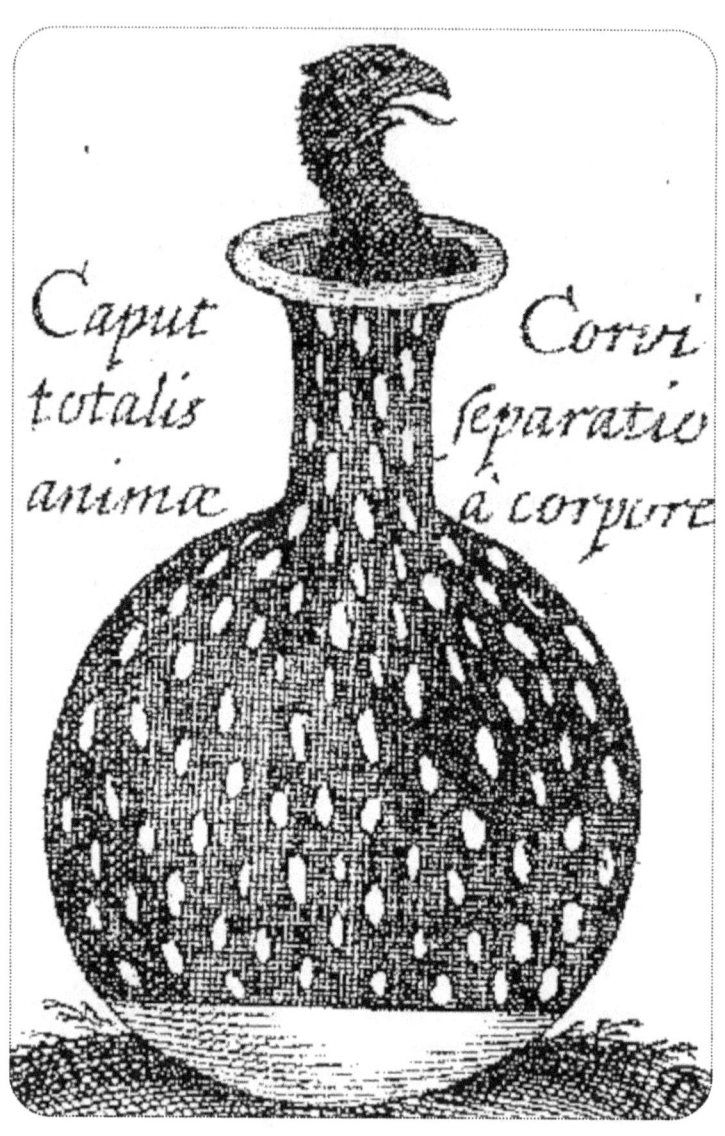

Engravings from J.D. Mylius' *Anatomia Auri*, 1628.

CHAPTER 7

PERSONAL TRANSFORMATIONS AND ALCHEMICAL SYMBOLISM

THE PHILOSOPHER'S STONE AS A METAPHOR FOR SELF-REALIZATION AND PERSONAL GROWTH

The Philosopher's Stone has long been revered as a physical object of transformation and a powerful metaphor for self-realization and personal growth. Throughout history, the quest for the Stone has symbolized the individual's inner journey, striving to achieve Enlightenment, self-knowledge, and spiritual wholeness.

In psychology, the Philosopher's Stone represents the ultimate goal of individuation—a concept central to Carl Jung's theories. Jung viewed alchemy as a symbolic language that mirrored the processes of the human psyche. He believed the alchemical quest was a metaphor for the individuation process, wherein individuals integrate different aspects of their personality to achieve a unified and balanced self.

The stages of alchemical transformation—nigredo (blackening), albedo (whitening), citrinitas (yellowing), and rubedo (reddening)—parallel the psychological processes of confronting the shadow, achieving clarity and insight, undergoing transformation, and reaching a state of wholeness. The Philosopher's Stone, in this context, symbolizes the attainment of self-realization, where the individual transcends inner conflicts and achieves a harmonious state of being.

The idea of the Philosopher's Stone as a metaphor for personal growth extends to various contemporary practices that emphasize self-improvement, mindfulness, and holistic well-being. In these practices, the journey toward the Stone is seen as an ongoing process of self-discovery, where individuals strive to overcome their limitations, unlock their potential, and achieve a more profound understanding of themselves and the world around them.

CONTEMPORARY ALCHEMICAL PRACTICES AND THEIR PSYCHOLOGICAL SIGNIFICANCE

Modern interpretations of alchemy have given rise to contemporary practices that draw on alchemical symbolism to promote psychological and spiritual growth. These practices, often called "psychological alchemy" or "inner alchemy," utilize the principles of alchemical transformation to facilitate personal development and healing.

One central tenet of contemporary alchemical practices is transforming the "lead" within oneself—symbolizing negative emotions, limiting beliefs, and unresolved traumas —into "gold," representing positive qualities, insights, and a sense of inner peace. Practitioners use techniques such as meditation, visualization, and creative expression to explore and transform their inner landscape.

In psychotherapy, alchemical symbolism is used to help clients understand and navigate their psychological processes. Therapists may employ alchemical metaphors to illustrate the stages of personal transformation and to provide clients with a framework for understanding their experiences. For example, the nigredo stage, characterized by confusion and darkness, can help clients recognize and work through periods of depression or existential crisis. In contrast, the albedo stage, associated with purification and clarity, can represent moments of insight and healing.

Contemporary spiritual practices also incorporate alchemical principles to promote holistic well-being. Yoga, qigong, and Reiki use inner alchemy to balance the body's energies and facilitate spiritual growth. These practices emphasize the interconnectedness of mind, body, and spirit, reflecting the alchemical belief in the unity of all things.

In addition to individual practices, modern alchemical groups and societies continue to explore and teach the principles of alchemy. These groups often blend traditional alchemical knowledge with contemporary psychological and spiritual insights, offering workshops, courses, and retreats focusing on personal transformation and self-discovery. Participants are encouraged to engage in reflective practices, study alchemical texts, and apply alchemical principles to their daily lives.

The enduring appeal of the Philosopher's Stone as a metaphor for self-realization and personal growth highlights the universal quest for transformation and Enlightenment. Contemporary alchemical practices, emphasizing inner transformation and holistic well-being, continue to draw on traditional alchemy's rich symbolism and philosophical insights.

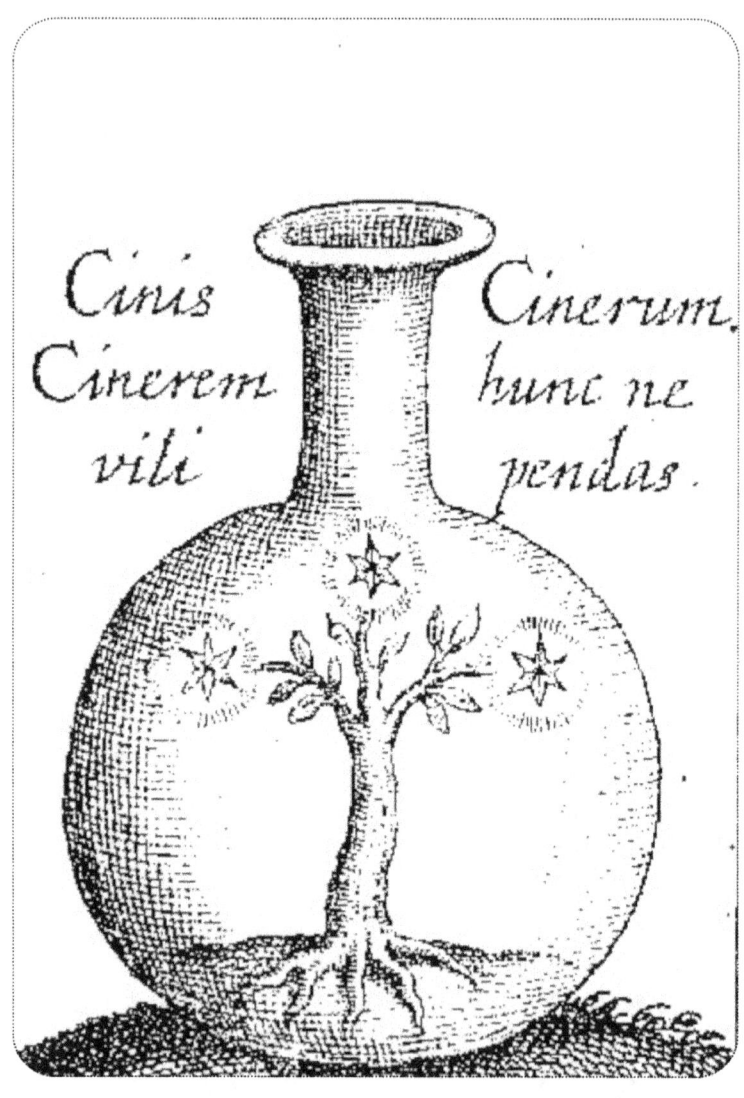

Engravings from J.D. Mylius' *Anatomia Auri,* 1628.

CHAPTER 8
ALCHEMISTS WHO MAY HAVE SUCCEEDED

NICOLAS FLAMEL: LEGEND AND LEGACY

Background
Nicolas Flamel, born in the mid-14th century in Paris, was a humble scribe and manuscript seller who became one of the most famous alchemists in history. Little is known about his early life, but records indicate that he was a learned man, well-versed in the languages and texts of his time. Flamel lived during a tremendous intellectual and cultural transformation, which may have influenced his interest in alchemical studies.

Alchemical Journey

The legend of Nicolas Flamel's discovery of the Philosopher's Stone begins with his acquisition of a mysterious alchemical book. According to the stories, Flamel came into possession of an ancient manuscript written in a cryptic language and filled with symbolic illustrations. Determined to decipher its secrets, Flamel sought the help of scholars and eventually traveled to Spain, where he met a Jewish scholar who helped him interpret the text.

Upon returning to Paris, Flamel reportedly began a series of alchemical experiments, culminating in the successful creation of the Philosopher's Stone. According to legend, this Stone enabled Flamel to transmute base metals into gold and produce the Elixir of Life, granting him and his wife, Perenelle, extraordinary longevity.

Legacy

Flamel's reputed success brought him immense wealth, which he and Perenelle used to fund charitable works. They financed the construction of churches, hospitals, and housing for the poor, actions that earned them great respect and admiration. Flamel's tomb in the Church of Saint-Jacques-la-Boucherie in Paris became a pilgrimage site for those interested in alchemy and the occult.

The posthumous legends surrounding Flamel grew, fueled by his association with the Philosopher's Stone. Many believed that Flamel and his wife had faked their deaths to live in secret, perpetually youthful and wealthy, thanks to the Elixir of Life.

Modern Interpretations

Nicolas Flamel's story has been immortalized in literature and media, where he is often depicted as the archetypal alchemist. He appears in Victor Hugo's "The Hunchback of Notre-Dame," where his house is described in detail. More recently, J.K. Rowling's "Harry Potter and the Philosopher's

Stone" (or "Sorcerer's Stone" in the U.S.) introduced Flamel to a new generation, portraying him as the creator of the Stone that grants immortality. These modern interpretations have cemented Flamel's legacy as a legendary figure in the annals of alchemy.

BASIL VALENTINE: DISCOVERIES AND MYSTERIES

Historical Context

Basil Valentine, a 15th-century Benedictine monk, is another enigmatic figure in the history of alchemy. His true identity remains a mystery, with some historians suggesting that "Basil Valentine" may have been a pseudonym used by a group of alchemists. Despite the uncertainty behind his identity, Valentine's contributions to alchemy were significant and enduring.

Contributions to Alchemy

Valentine is best known for his written works, particularly "The Twelve Keys," a series of alchemical texts describing alchemical transmutation processes and stages. These works are characterized by their rich symbolism and allegorical language, making them both fascinating and challenging for modern readers.

"The Twelve Keys" outlines the steps necessary to achieve the Magnum Opus, or Great Work, of alchemy—the creation of the Philosopher's Stone. Valentine's detailed descriptions of the alchemical processes, including distillation, calcination, and sublimation, provided valuable insights for subsequent generations of alchemists.

Philosopher's Stone

There is anecdotal evidence and claims suggesting that Basil Valentine succeeded in creating the Philosopher's Stone. Some historical accounts describe Valentine as possessing profound knowledge of alchemical transmutation and achieving remarkable successes in his experiments. However, these claims remain speculative and often intertwine with the myth and mysticism surrounding alchemy.

Valentine's work had a lasting impact on the development of alchemy and influenced many later alchemists. Those interested in the alchemical tradition's philosophical and practical aspects continue to study his writings.

COUNT OF ST. GERMAIN: THE IMMORTAL ALCHEMIST

Enigmatic Figure

The Count of St. Germain, an 18th-century European courtier, diplomat, and alchemist, is one of alchemical lore's most enigmatic and fascinating figures. His origins and true identity are shrouded in mystery, and much of what is known about him comes from accounts and anecdotes that blend fact and fiction.

Immortality and Alchemy

St. Germain was reputed to possess extraordinary knowledge and abilities. He was known for his linguistic skills, musical talent, and scientific knowledge. However, his alleged immortality and alchemical prowess made him a legendary figure. According to various accounts, St. Germain claimed to have discovered the secret of eternal youth and the Philosopher's Stone, allowing him to live without aging for centuries.

The Count's longevity and mysterious background fueled speculation that he had succeeded in creating the Philosopher's Stone. Some reports suggest that he was seen in various European courts over many decades, seemingly unchanged by time. These stories contributed to the belief that St. Germain had unlocked the secrets of alchemical transmutation and immortality.

Influence and Legacy

St. Germain's influence extended beyond alchemy. He was a trusted advisor to several European monarchs and played a role in diplomatic and political affairs. His reputation as an alchemist and his enigmatic persona made him a subject of fascination in esoteric traditions.

In modern times, St. Germain is often depicted as a master of esoteric knowledge and a symbol of the pursuit of eternal wisdom. He appears in various occult and mystical traditions, including Theosophy and New Age spirituality, where he is venerated as an ascended master. St. Germain's legacy as the "Immortal Alchemist" continues to captivate those interested in the mysteries of alchemy and the quest for immortality.

PARACELSUS: TRANSFORMATIVE PRACTICES AND BELIEFS

Life and Works

Paracelsus, born Philippus Aureolus Theophrastus Bombastus von Hohenheim in 1493, was a Swiss physician, alchemist, and philosopher who profoundly influenced medicine and alchemy. Paracelsus challenged the medical orthodoxy of his time, advocating for a holistic approach to health and healing that integrated alchemical principles.

Paracelsus traveled extensively, gathering knowledge from various cultures and traditions. His work emphasized the importance of understanding substances' properties and their effects on the human body. He introduced the concept of "spagyria," an alchemical process that involved the extraction, purification, and recombination of medicinal substances.

Alchemical Philosophy

Paracelsus believed in the transformative powers of alchemy, both in terms of physical substances and the human spirit. He viewed alchemy as a means of understanding the hidden properties of nature and harnessing them for healing and personal transformation. Paracelsus's alchemical philosophy was grounded in the idea that the microcosm (the individual) reflected the macrocosm (the universe) and that by mastering the principles of alchemy, one could achieve harmony and balance within oneself.

Philosopher's Stone

There are claims that Paracelsus succeeded in creating the Philosopher's Stone. However, these claims are often shrouded in legend and mysticism. Paracelsus's writings suggest that he believed in the possibility of transmutation and the creation of the Stone, which he saw as the culmination of the alchemical process. However, his focus was primarily on alchemy's medicinal and spiritual applications rather than the pursuit of wealth through the transmutation of metals.

Paracelsus's broader impact on alchemical thought and medicine was profound. His emphasis on empirical observation, using natural remedies, and integrating alchemical principles into medical practice laid the groundwork for modern pharmacology and holistic medicine.

The lives and works of Nicolas Flamel, Basil Valentine, the Count of St. Germain, and Paracelsus highlight the enduring fascination with the Philosopher's Stone and the quest for alchemical transformation. Through actual achievements or the legends that grew around them, these alchemists contributed to the rich tapestry of the alchemical tradition. Their stories continue to inspire and intrigue, reflecting the timeless human desire for knowledge, transformation, and the pursuit of the extraordinary.

As we conclude our exploration of the history and modern interpretations of the Philosopher's Stone, we see how this ancient symbol has evolved and persisted, reflecting the enduring human quest for transformation and Enlightenment.

In the final chapter, we will summarize our journey's key themes and insights, reflecting on the timeless appeal and universal significance of the Philosopher's Stone in the ongoing pursuit of knowledge and self-discovery.

Engravings from J.D. Mylius' *Anatomia Auri*, 1628.

CHAPTER 9
END OF THE JOURNEY

SUMMARY OF THE HISTORICAL JOURNEY AND MODERN INTERPRETATIONS

The Philosopher's Stone, an elusive and enigmatic symbol, has captivated human imagination for centuries. Our journey through its history has taken us from the ancient temples of Egypt and the philosophical schools of Greece to the bustling centers of Islamic learning and the secretive laboratories of medieval Europe. We have seen how the quest for the Stone was driven by scientific curiosity, spiritual aspiration, and the human desire for mastery over nature.

Alchemical practices were deeply intertwined with religious and philosophical beliefs in Ancient Egypt and Greece. The concept of chrysopoeia, or the transformation of base metals into gold, symbolized material wealth and spiritual perfection. This early foundation set the stage for the rich alchemical traditions that followed.

During the Islamic Golden Age, scholars like Jabir ibn Hayyan and Al-Razi advanced alchemical knowledge through rigorous experimentation and synthesis of Greek and Egyptian wisdom. Their contributions laid crucial groundwork for later European developments, demonstrating how alchemy served as a bridge between ancient and medieval sciences.

The medieval period saw alchemy flourish in Europe, where figures like Albertus Magnus, Roger Bacon, and Nicolas Flamel became legends in their own right. Their stories, whether grounded in historical fact or myth, fueled the pursuit of the Philosopher's Stone to achieve both material transmutation and spiritual Enlightenment.

The Renaissance and Enlightenment revived alchemical interests, with Hermeticism adding a mystical dimension to the quest. Alchemists like Paracelsus integrated alchemical principles into medicine, emphasizing the transformative power of nature and the interconnectedness of the macrocosm and microcosm. This period also marked a shift from physical to spiritual alchemy, reflecting broader changes in philosophical and scientific thought.

In modern times, the Philosopher's Stone continues to inspire and intrigue. Its presence in literature, popular culture, and contemporary spiritual practices underscores its enduring appeal. Figures like Nicolas Flamel and the Count of St. Germain have been immortalized in books and films, illustrating how the myth of the Stone remains relevant and compelling.

THE ENDURING LEGACY OF THE PHILOSOPHER'S STONE

The legacy of the Philosopher's Stone is multifaceted and profound. It represents the human spirit's relentless pursuit of transformation and perfection, embodying the desire to transcend the ordinary and achieve the extraordinary. This quest is reflected in the numerous legends, texts, and practices that have emerged over the centuries, each contributing to the rich tapestry of the alchemical tradition.

In science, alchemists' rigorous methodologies and experimental techniques laid essential foundations for modern chemistry and medicine. The transition from alchemy to chemistry, driven by figures like Antoine Lavoisier, marked a critical evolution in our understanding of the natural world. The principles of empirical observation and systematic experimentation, hallmarks of alchemical practice, continue to underpin scientific inquiry today.

Spiritually and philosophically, the Philosopher's Stone symbolizes the quest for inner transformation and Enlightenment. Alchemical metaphors resonate deeply in contemporary psychological and spiritual practices, exploring the processes of personal growth, healing, and self-discovery. The Stone's symbolism as a catalyst for inner alchemy—transforming one's "lead" into "gold"—remains a powerful tool for understanding the journey toward wholeness and self-realization.

FINAL REFLECTIONS ON THE HUMAN QUEST FOR TRANSFORMATION AND ENLIGHTENMENT

The story of the Philosopher's Stone is, at its heart, about the human quest for transformation and Enlightenment. It reflects our innate drive to explore, understand, and transcend the limitations of our existence. Whether through the lens of ancient mythology, medieval alchemical practice, or modern scientific and spiritual exploration, the pursuit of the Stone symbolizes a universal and timeless aspiration.

This aspiration is not just about achieving material wealth or physical immortality but the more profound desire to uncover the hidden truths of the universe and ourselves. The alchemists' belief in the unity of the material and spiritual realms and their quest to transform both speak to a profound recognition of the interconnectedness of all things.

As we reflect on the journey through the history and modern interpretations of the Philosopher's Stone, we see that this symbol continues to inspire and challenge us. It calls us to look beyond the surface, to seek a deeper understanding, and to embrace the transformative potential within us. The Philosopher's Stone, whether viewed as a literal substance or a metaphorical ideal, represents the enduring human quest for knowledge, growth, and enlightenment.

In conclusion, the Philosopher's Stone is a testament to the power of the human spirit. It reminds us that the journey of transformation is as important as the destination, and that the pursuit of Enlightenment is a timeless and universal endeavor. As we continue to explore and expand our understanding, the legacy of the Philosopher's Stone will undoubtedly remain a guiding light on our path toward self-realization and ultimate knowledge.

Engravings from J.D. Mylius' *Anatomia Auri*, 1628.

APPENDIX

THE EMERALD TABLET OF HERMES

The Emerald Tablet of Hermes Trismegistus is one of the most revered and enigmatic texts in the history of alchemy. Often considered the foundation of Western alchemical thought, this concise yet profound document encapsulates the essence of the alchemical process and the quest for the Philosopher's Stone. Its cryptic verses have been interpreted and reinterpreted by countless alchemists, philosophers, and mystics, each finding new layers of meaning within its timeless words. Here, we will explore the contents of the Emerald Tablet and its correlation with the Philosopher's Stone and highlight key passages for a more profound understanding.

The Text of the Emerald Tablet

True, without falsehood, certain, and most true.

That which is below is like that which is above, and that which is above is like that which is below, to accomplish the miracles of one thing.

And as all things have been and arose from one by the meditation of one, so all things have their birth from this one thing by adaptation.

Its father is the Sun, its mother the Moon; the wind hath carried it in its belly, the earth is its nurse.

The father of all perfection in the whole world is here.

Its force or power is entire if it be converted into earth.

Separate thou the earth from the fire, the subtle from the gross sweetly with great industry.

It ascends from the earth to the heaven, and again it descends to the earth, and receives the force of things superior and inferior.

By this means you shall have the glory of the whole world, and thereby all obscurity shall fly from you.

*Its force is above all force, for it vanquishes every
    subtle thing and penetrates every solid thing.
So was the world created.*

*From this are and do come admirable adapta-
    tions whereof the means (or process) is here
    in this.*

*Hence I am called Hermes Trismegistus, having
    the three parts of the philosophy of the whole
    world.*

*That which I have said of the operation of the
    Sun is accomplished and ended.*

CORRELATION WITH THE PHILOSOPHER'S STONE

The Emerald Tablet is intrinsically linked to the
Philosopher's Stone because it describes the alchemical
process and the principles underlying transformation. The
Tablet's verses outline the fundamental truths and opera-
tions necessary for achieving the Great Work, or Magnum
Opus, of alchemy.

1. "True, without falsehood, certain, and most true."

- **Annotation:** This opening statement
  emphasizes the absolute certainty and
  authenticity of the knowledge contained within
  the Tablet, reinforcing its importance and
  authority.

2. "That which is below is like that which is above, and that which is above is like that which is below, to accomplish the miracles of one thing."

- **Annotation**: This Hermetic axiom, "As above, so below," highlights the correspondence principle. It suggests that the processes and transformations occurring in the macrocosm (the universe) are reflected in the microcosm (the individual).

This concept is crucial for understanding how the alchemical process mirrors the spiritual journey of the alchemist.

3. "And as all things have been and arose from one by the meditation of one, so all things have their birth from this one thing by adaptation."

- **Annotation**: This verse points to the unity of all creation, originating from a single source. In the context of alchemy, this "one thing" is often interpreted as the prima materia, the raw material from which the Philosopher's Stone is created.

4. "Its father is the Sun, its mother the Moon; the wind hath carried it in its belly, the earth is its nurse."

- **Annotation**: The alchemical symbols of the Sun (gold) and Moon (silver) represent masculine and feminine principles. The wind and earth symbolize the essential elements required for the alchemical process. This verse illustrates the harmonious balance of opposing forces necessary for creation.

5. "The father of all perfection in the whole world is here."

- **Annotation**: This statement indicates that the secret of perfection and the ultimate goal of alchemy, the Philosopher's Stone, is encapsulated within the teachings of the Tablet.

6. "Its force or power is entire if it be converted into earth."

- **Annotation**: This line emphasizes the importance of grounding the spiritual insights gained through alchemy into practical, tangible reality. It suggests that the true power of the Philosopher's Stone is realized when it is made manifest in the physical world.

7. "Separate thou the earth from the fire, the subtle from the gross sweetly with great industry."

- **Annotation**: This directive instructs the alchemist to distinguish and separate the pure from the impure elements. It symbolizes the purification process essential for creating the Philosopher's Stone.

8. "It ascends from the earth to the heaven, and again it descends to the earth, and receives the force of things superior and inferior."

- **Annotation:** This verse describes the cyclical nature of the alchemical process, where the matter is repeatedly purified and elevated, integrating the energies of both the higher and lower realms.

9. "By this means you shall have the glory of the whole world, and thereby all obscurity shall fly from you."

- **Annotation:** Achieving the Philosopher's Stone grants the alchemist profound knowledge and enlightenment, dispelling ignorance and darkness.

10. "Its force is above all force, for it vanquishes every subtle thing and penetrates every solid thing."

- **Annotation:** The Philosopher's Stone possesses unparalleled power, capable of transforming and perfecting all subtle and gross substances.

11. "So was the world created."

- **Annotation:** This statement links the alchemical process to the act of creation itself, suggesting that the principles of alchemy mirror the fundamental processes of the cosmos.

12. "From this are and do come admirable adaptations whereof the means (or process) is here in this."

- **Annotation:** This verse highlights the adaptability and versatility of alchemical principles applicable to various aspects of transformation and creation.

13. "Hence I am called Hermes Trismegistus, having the three parts of the philosophy of the whole world."

- **Annotation:** Legendary figure Hermes Trismegistus is associated with the synthesis of alchemy, astrology, and theurgy. This line underscores the comprehensive nature of his teachings.

14. "That which I have said of the operation of the Sun is accomplished and ended."

- **Annotation:** The concluding statement signifies the completion of the alchemical process, where the operation of the Sun (gold) symbolizes the successful creation of the Philosopher's Stone.

The Emerald Tablet of Hermes Trismegistus offers a profound and poetic encapsulation of the alchemical quest for the Philosopher's Stone. Its verses provide practical guidance and deep philosophical insights into the nature of transformation and the unity of all things. By understanding and applying the principles outlined in the Tablet, alchemists sought to achieve material transmutation, spiritual enlightenment, and perfection.

The correlations between the Emerald Tablet and the Philosopher's Stone underscore the interconnectedness of the alchemical tradition, where physical processes mirror spiritual journeys, and the ultimate goal is the realization of the divine within the material world. The Tablet's enduring legacy inspires and guides seekers on their path to knowledge and transformation, reflecting the timeless and universal nature of the alchemical quest.

ALCHEMICAL SYMBOLS AND THEIR MEANINGS

Alchemical symbolism is a complex and rich language used by alchemists to encode their knowledge, practices, and spiritual insights. These symbols, often enigmatic and multi-layered, provided a means of communication and protection for esoteric knowledge. In this chapter, we will explore the most significant alchemical symbols, their meanings, and their roles within the alchemical tradition. Understanding these symbols offers a window into the mindset and philosophies of alchemists and reveals the profound interplay between material and spiritual transformation in their work.

The Three Principles

1. **Sulfur (♠)**
   - **Symbolism**: Sulfur represents the active, fiery principle, associated with the soul and spiritual essence. It is linked to the qualities of combustibility and volatility.

- **Alchemical Processes**: Sulfur is seen as the transforming agent that drives change and metamorphosis in the alchemical process. It embodies the qualities of desire, will, and the dynamic forces of nature.
- **Philosophical Meaning**: Sulfur's transformative power is essential in purifying and perfecting the base materials, contributing to the creation of the Philosopher's Stone.

2. **Mercury ($\mathint{\mathrm{\breve{\text{}}}}$)**
   - **Symbolism**: Mercury represents the fluid, volatile principle, associated with the mind and the spirit. It is linked to the qualities of adaptability and changeability.
   - **Alchemical Processes**: Mercury acts as the mediator between Sulfur and Salt, facilitating the union of opposites. It symbolizes the mind's ability to perceive and adapt to new forms and ideas.
   - **Philosophical Meaning**: Mercury's ability to amalgamate and harmonize different elements is crucial in achieving the cohesive and transformative properties of the Philosopher's Stone.

3. **Salt (⊖)**
   - **Symbolism**: Salt represents the stable, solid principle, associated with the body and material substance. It is linked to the qualities of preservation and crystallization.

- **Alchemical Processes**: Salt provides the structural integrity and stability needed for the alchemical transformation. It embodies the qualities of endurance and resilience.
- **Philosophical Meaning**: Salt's stabilizing influence is vital for grounding the transformative energies of Sulfur and Mercury, leading to the final crystallization of the Philosopher's Stone.

The Four Elements

1. **Fire ($\triangle$)**
   - **Symbolism**: Fire represents energy, transformation, and purification. It is associated with the process of calcination, where substances are heated to high temperatures to remove impurities.
   - **Alchemical Processes**: Calcination, combustion, and the beginning of transformation.
   - **Philosophical Meaning**: Fire symbolizes the fiery nature of spirit and the active principle in the universe. It is also connected to the willpower and determination needed for the alchemical work.

2. **Water (∇)**
   - **Symbolism**: Water signifies intuition, emotion, and the fluidity of life. It is used in alchemical processes like dissolution and purification.

- **Alchemical Processes**: Dissolution, distillation, and the purification of substances.
- **Philosophical Meaning**: Water represents the unconscious mind, the flow of life, and the potential for transformation through emotional and intuitive understanding.

3. **Earth (▽)**
   - **Symbolism**: Earth stands for stability, materiality, and the physical aspect of existence. It is associated with the processes of coagulation and crystallization.
   - **Alchemical Processes**: Coagulation, crystallization, and the grounding of transformed substances.
   - **Philosophical Meaning**: Earth symbolizes the grounding of spiritual insights into physical reality and the manifestation of spiritual goals in the material world.

4. **Air (△)**
   - **Symbolism**: Air represents intellect, communication, and the breath of life. It is linked to the processes of sublimation and transformation of matter into spirit.
   - **Alchemical Processes**: Sublimation, separation, and the elevation of material substances.
   - **Philosophical Meaning**: Air signifies the mind's ability to grasp and articulate

spiritual truths and the elevation of thought towards higher understanding.

The Seven Metals and Their Planetary Associations

1. **Gold (Sun ☉)**
   - **Symbolism**: Gold represents perfection, enlightenment, and the divine spirit. It is the ultimate goal of alchemical transmutation.
   - **Philosophical Meaning**: Gold symbolizes the perfection of the soul and the attainment of spiritual enlightenment.

2. **Silver (Moon ☽)**
   - **Symbolism**: Silver signifies purity, clarity, and the reflective nature of the soul.
   - **Philosophical Meaning**: Silver represents the pure, receptive aspect of the soul, reflecting higher truths and spiritual insights.

3. **Mercury (Mercury ☿)**
   - **Symbolism**: Mercury embodies fluidity, adaptability, and transformation. It is seen as both a metal and a planet, representing the alchemical principle of change.
   - **Philosophical Meaning**: Mercury symbolizes the mind's ability to transform and adapt, acting as a mediator between the physical and spiritual realms.

4. **Copper (Venus ♀)**

- **Symbolism**: Copper represents love, harmony, and artistic creativity.
- **Philosophical Meaning**: Copper symbolizes the unifying force of love and beauty, facilitating the harmony and balance necessary for spiritual growth.

5. **Iron (Mars ♂)**
   - **Symbolism**: Iron signifies strength, willpower, and the warrior spirit.
   - **Philosophical Meaning**: Iron represents the strength and determination needed to overcome obstacles and drive the alchemical process forward.

6. **Tin (Jupiter ♃)**
   - **Symbolism**: Tin stands for expansion, wisdom, and growth.
   - **Philosophical Meaning**: Tin symbolizes the expansive nature of wisdom and the growth that comes from spiritual and intellectual pursuits.

7. **Lead (Saturn ♄)**
   - **Symbolism**: Lead represents heaviness, limitation, and the prima materia (base matter) from which transformation begins.
   - **Philosophical Meaning**: Lead symbolizes the starting point of the alchemical journey, representing the material and spiritual impurities that must be transformed.

The 12 stages of the alchemical process

1. **Calcination:**
   o **Meaning:** The stage of burning or heating a substance until it is reduced to ashes. Calcination represents the destruction of the ego and the material aspects of the self.

2. **Dissolution:**
   o **Meaning:** Dissolving the ashes in water symbolizes the breakdown of artificial constructs and the ego, leading to a more fluid state of consciousness.

3. **Separation:**
   o **Meaning:** The isolation of different components of the substance. This stage represents the need to distinguish between the actual and false selves, separating impurities from the essence.

4. **Conjunction:**
   o **Meaning:** The recombination of the purified elements. Conjunction signifies the union of opposites, such as masculine and feminine or body and soul, leading to a harmonious whole.

5. **Fermentation:**
   o **Meaning:** The introduction of new life or spirit into the substance. This stage

represents spiritual awakening and the beginning of inner transformation.

6. **Distillation:**
   - ○ **Meaning:** Purifying the substance by heating and condensing it repeatedly. This process symbolizes the continual refinement of thoughts and emotions, leading to higher levels of consciousness.

7. **Coagulation:**
   - ○ **Meaning:** The solidification of the purified substance into a stable form. This stage represents the manifestation of the spiritual into the physical, achieving a state of enlightenment or the creation of the Philosopher's Stone.

8. **Sublimation:**
   - ○ **Meaning:** The process of changing a solid directly into a gas. This stage signifies the physical transformation into the spiritual, representing the soul's ascent.

9. **Mortification:**
   - ○ **Meaning:** The stage of decay and putrefaction, where the old form breaks down. Mortification symbolizes the death of old habits and ways of being, allowing new growth.

10. **Multiplication:**
    ○ **Meaning:** The increase in the quantity and quality of the elixir. This stage represents the enhancement and amplification of the transformative powers of the Philosopher's Stone.

11. **Projection:**
    ○ **Meaning:** The act of projecting the Philosopher's Stone onto a base metal to transmute it into gold. Projection symbolizes applying spiritual enlightenment to transform and perfect the material world.

12. **Fixation:**
    ○ **Meaning:** Stabilizing the elixir so that it can withstand fire without vaporizing. This stage represents the achievement of permanence and immortality, the ultimate goal of the alchemical process.

OTHER KEY SYMBOLS

- **The Philosopher's Stone**
    ○ **Symbolism:** The Philosopher's Stone represents the ultimate goal of alchemy, capable of transforming base metals into gold and granting immortality.
    ○ **Philosophical Meaning:** It symbolizes the perfected soul, spiritual enlightenment, and the attainment of divine wisdom.

- **The Ouroboros**
  - **Symbolism**: The Ouroboros is depicted as a serpent or dragon eating its own tail, symbolizing the cyclical nature of the alchemical process.
  - **Philosophical Meaning**: It represents the eternal cycle of creation and destruction, the unity of all things, and the concept of eternal return.

- **The Hermetic Seal**
  - **Symbolism**: Often depicted as a triangle within a circle, the Hermetic Seal represents the integration of the three principles (Sulfur, Mercury, Salt) in a harmonious unity.
  - **Philosophical Meaning**: It symbolizes the unity of opposites and the holistic nature of the alchemical work.

- **The Phoenix**
  - **Symbolism**: The Phoenix represents rebirth and renewal, rising from its own ashes.
  - **Philosophical Meaning**: It symbolizes the alchemical process of death and rebirth, the renewal of the spirit, and the attainment of immortality.

- **The Ankh**
  - **Symbolism**: An ancient Egyptian symbol representing life and immortality.

- **Philosophical Meaning**: It symbolizes the eternal nature of the soul and the alchemical quest for eternal life.

- **The Alembic**
  - **Symbolism**: A distillation apparatus used in alchemy.
  - **Philosophical Meaning**: It represents the process of purification and refinement of the soul.

- **The Athanor**
  - **Symbolism**: An alchemical furnace used to provide constant heat for processes.
  - **Philosophical Meaning**: It symbolizes the inner fire of spiritual aspiration and the sustained effort required for transformation.

GLOSSARY OF ALCHEMICAL TERMS

- **Albedo**: The second stage of the alchemical process, also known as "whitening." It represents purification and enlightenment.
- **Alchemy**: A philosophical and proto-scientific tradition aimed at transforming base metals into noble metals (like gold) and discovering the Elixir of Life.
- **Chrysopoeia**: The transmutation of base metals into gold, central to alchemical pursuits.
- **Citrinitas**: The third stage of the alchemical process, known as "yellowing." It represents the

dawning of the solar consciousness and the beginning of the transformation.

- **Distillation:** A purification process in alchemy where a liquid is heated to create vapor and then condensed back into liquid.
- **Elixir of Life:** A mythical substance believed to grant eternal life and perfect health.
- **Emerald Tablet:** A Hermetic text attributed to Hermes Trismegistus, summarizing the principles of alchemy.
- **Hermeticism:** A philosophical and spiritual tradition based on writings attributed to Hermes Trismegistus, emphasizing the unity of the material and spiritual worlds.
- **Nigredo:** The first stage of the alchemical process, also known as "blackening." It represents decomposition and the breaking down of impurities.
- **Philosopher's Stone:** A legendary substance in alchemy believed to enable the transmutation of base metals into gold and grant immortality.
- **Prima Materia:** The original, unformed substance from which all matter is believed to originate in alchemical theory.
- **Rubedo:** The final stage of the alchemical process, known as "reddening." It signifies the achievement of the Great Work and the creation of the Philosopher's Stone.
- **Spagyria:** The alchemical preparation of medicinal substances, involving the processes of separation, purification, and recombination.

- **Transmutation**: The alchemical process of transforming one substance into another, particularly base metals into gold.

TIMELINE OF KEY EVENTS

- **Circa 3000 BCE**: Early metallurgical practices in Ancient Egypt, laying the groundwork for alchemical traditions.
- **Circa 600 BCE**: Greek philosophers, such as Thales and Pythagoras, explore the nature of matter and the concept of transformation.
- **Circa 200 CE**: Publication of the "Emerald Tablet," attributed to Hermes Trismegistus.
- **Circa 800-900 CE**: Islamic Golden Age; contributions of alchemists like Jabir ibn Hayyan and Al-Razi.
- **Circa 1200-1300 CE**: Medieval European alchemists such as Albertus Magnus and Roger Bacon advance alchemical knowledge.
- **Circa 1378-1418 CE**: Life and legend of Nicolas Flamel, reputed discoverer of the Philosopher's Stone.
- **Circa 1410-1500 CE**: Basil Valentine's contributions to alchemy, including "The Twelve Keys."
- **Circa 1493-1541 CE**: Life of Paracelsus, who integrates alchemy with medicine and holistic healing.
- **Circa 1700-1784 CE**: Count of St. Germain, an

enigmatic figure associated with immortality and alchemical mastery.

- **Late 18th Century**: Antoine Lavoisier's work in chemistry, debunking traditional alchemical transmutation.
- **1869 CE**: Dmitri Mendeleev publishes the periodic table, categorizing elements and challenging alchemical concepts.
- **20th Century**: Carl Jung's exploration of alchemy as a metaphor for psychological processes.

RECOMMENDED READING AND RESOURCES FOR FURTHER STUDY

- **Books:**
  - **"The Alchemist" by Paulo Coelho**: A novel that uses alchemical themes to explore personal transformation and the pursuit of one's dreams.
  - **"The Chemical Choir: A History of Alchemy" by P.G. Maxwell-Stuart**: A comprehensive history of alchemy from ancient times to the modern era.
  - **"Alchemical Studies" by Carl Jung**: An exploration of alchemical symbolism and its psychological significance.
  - **"The Hermetic Tradition: Symbols and Teachings of the Royal Art" by Julius Evola**: A detailed study of Hermeticism and its influence on alchemical practices.

- "The Philosopher's Stone: A Quest for the Secrets of Alchemy" by Peter Marshall: An engaging account of the history and mysteries of alchemy and the Philosopher's Stone.

- **Academic Journals and Articles:**
  - "Ambix: The Journal of the Society for the History of Alchemy and Chemistry": An academic journal dedicated to the study of the history of alchemy and chemistry.
  - "Alchemy in Context: The Rebirth of Alchemy in the Renaissance": A scholarly article exploring the revival of alchemy during the Renaissance.

- **Documentaries and Films:**
  - "The Mystery of Alchemy" (BBC Documentary): An informative documentary exploring the history and legacy of alchemy.
  - "Alchemy: Sacred Secrets Revealed": A film that delves into the mystical and philosophical aspects of alchemy.

Engravings from J.D. Mylius' *Anatomia Auri*, 1628.

THE TREATISE "SIX CHAPTERS"

The treatise known as "Six Chapters" is anonymous yet profoundly influential within the rich tapestry of alchemical literature. Included in Elias Ashmole's seminal collection, "Theatrum Chemicum Britannicum," it serves as a comprehensive guide to both the mystical and practical aspects of alchemy, with a particular focus on the creation and utilization of the Philosopher's Stone.

FIRST CHAPTER.

IN the name of the holy Trinitie,
    I will write of this Worke breiflie;
    Leaving matters of circumstance,
    And promise the truth to advance:
    I will not write Figuratively,
    But declare the Matter plainely,
    And how things must be made to accord,
    By Natures true worke and the helpe of our Lord:
    The World is but one inclosed with heavens round,

Though divers matters and formes be therein found:
The Earth this worlds Center borne up by the Aire,
In kinde hath noe more but being baire,
And neerest to not being, Philosophers have told,
In kinde of Complexion is full dry and cold;
And now for my Figure of rotundity,
I will shew how Elements accord and disagree:
And though the Elements be so contrary,
Yett by heavens Influence they are brought to unite,
And when once togeather a body they binde,
Nought may them loosen without wrecke to the kinde.
First Fire in Nature is hott and dry,
Aire differs from Fire in moisture only :
Earth only for coldnesse from Fire disagrees,
This Concord and discord every man sees:
Aire hot and moist of complexion and kinde,
Water differs from Aire but in heate we finde:
Soe that in moysture we finde them both one:
Naturall heate in Water we finde none;
Water cold and moiste of Complexion is,
Earth differs from Water in drynes I wis :
Earth agrees with Fire in drynes noe doubte,
Thus one in another the Wheele turnes about.
From this round Circle proceeds a quadrant,
Each line unto another an equall distant:
And as the round Figure concludes all in One,
Soe the Quadrant of foure things makes distinction.
From this Quadrant a Fire must proceed,
Which is *Animall*, *Vegitable* and *Minerall* we reede:
And with the Fire I will begin;
Pray God I be not too bold therein.
The whole Composition of this world is fram'd

Of the Three things which before I have nam'd:
Now to make things of Excellencie,
We must take things neerest Nobilitie;
And as this greate Masse conteines things Three,
Soe Blood, Flesh and Bone in the least World we see;
Yett lesse World and greate World is all but One;
Thus still we keepe an Unyon:
Whatsoever itt is that is alive,
Without Blood they may not thrive.
Sperme is Generacion of each thing,
Of what kinde soever itt bene;
Blood is Sperme be itt White or Redd,
For without Blood each thing is dead:
Blood conteineth the three things I have told,
And in his Tincture hath Nature of Gold:
Without Gold noe Mettle may shine bright,
Without Blood noe Body hath bene fitt of light:
Thus doth the greate and lesse World still,
Hold the Union according to Gods will:
Now of all things Blood Noblest is,
For nothing in the World may itt misse,
Blood hath true proporcion of the Elements foure,
And of the three species I spoke of before:
The Blood must be the principall matter of each thing,
Which hath any manner of increasing :
Mercury in Mettalls is the Blood certeine,
Sperme in Animalls getts the like againe;
Vegetable moysture from heaven so good,
Yett all these three are but Blood :
Then Blood in procreation is neerest of kinde,
This Secrett good Brother keepe close in thy mynde:
And uppon that Condition,

Which Blood thou shalt take I will make repeticion;
The true Blood of Mettalls is hard to have,
And long tyme of getting itt doth crave:
Blood of Vegetables hath moysture greate store,
And therefore to have itt requireth much labour:
The true Blood to finde without labour and cost,
Thou knowst where to have it ere thy witts be lost.
Seeke out the noblest as I said before,
For now of the Matter I dare say noe more.
This Secrett was never reveal'd till this tyme,
By any Mans writings that ere I could finde,
But I which by practice have found itt true,
Knew how things caused things to renew:
God grant noe *Alchymists* meete with my Booke,
For they would have Elixir by hooke or by crooke;
And he would spend what his Freinds wan,
And be as neere at the last as when he began,
And would promise to give men Gold greate store,
But beware thou of Expence, as I said before.

CHAP. II. OF THE MANNER OF THE WORKE.

NOW after the Matter the Manner compute,
    How to bring this our Worke aboute:
    First take the Matter crude as itt is,
    Which will cost you little or nought I wis :
    Searce it soe cleane as it may be,
    Untill from filth itt is all free,
    Which wilbee done in houres three or foure,
    Then will it be cleare from his ill humour:
    Then take the Faces which you shall finde,
    In the same which the Matter left behind:

Purge him also with the noblest Element,
Untill that he to Earth be brent:
Then have you a *Stone* of wonderfull might,
With small Cost a secret right.
Take ye this *Stone* and use Millers Craft,
Till it be fine powder and made very soft:
Then give him the moisture which from him ye tooke,
Then use him as ye shall finde in this booke.
But give him noe other Drinke but of his owne kinde,
For elce you doe not after my mynde.
Let him drinke noe more then will suffice,
Beware of Floods I you advise:
Then search him twice againe as you did before,
And still put uppon his owne liquor:
Thus their first Order to passe is brought,
And your foulest Worke fully wrought.

CHAP. III. OF THE SECOND ORDER.

NOW the second Manner I will shew plaine,
How you shall worke it with little paine:
When your three searsings be done after my lore,
Then breake the *Stone* as you did before:
Then must you have on Veschell,
Which must be made like an Eggshell,
Into the which Vessell the Matter you must putt,
Then see that itt be well closed upp:
The Vessells divided in parts three,
Whereof two still voyde must bee:
This Vessell must be set in a kinde heate,
That the Matter may kindly sweate;
The Spiritts must not be opprest with Fire,

For then thou shalt never have thy desire;
Neither must thy Vessell have cold,
For then itt will spoile as *Philosophers* have told;
But keepe itt in a temperate heate alwayes,
For the space of fortie dayes:
Then Blackesse will appeare to sight,
That Blacknesse thou must bring to be White.
ake out the Glasse at the forty dayes end,
And se that from cold thou doe itt defend;
And set itt in a Furnace with dry fire,
Till itt be White after thy desire,
Which wilbe done in Weekes three,
And dryed from his moysture utterly :
Then with the first Water thou first didst imbibe
Againe thou maist feede it att this tyde,
But give itt noe more, nor you doe thinke
May suffice at once for itt to drinke,
This done putrefy as you did before,
Even in the very selfe same maner,
And in the said tyme which it stoode before,
Itt will becom of blacke Colour,
And in the same Order if it congeale White,
Then is your Worke both perfect and right;
Now you must goe lerne the Bakers occupacion,
How he Leavens Bread by Fermentacion;
And truly to Ferment take noe plate of Gold,
But parte of that the plates doe hold.
You know that if *Sol* shew not a faire Tincture,
Itt will be had but in little honour,
Then Tincture of Gold is a most noble thing,
With a grace to noble men of our workeing,
For that true proverbe doth well accord,

Base things befitt not a noble Lord.
Now have I told you what Ferment is,
To teach you to Ferment I will not misse;
This Chapter is now brought to an end,
And now the third Order to shew I intend.

CHAP. IV. OF THE THIRD ORDER OF THIS WORKE.

RECIPE *Sol* that is pure and good,
    And see that from him you take his pure blood,
    Your *Stone* you must divide in parts three,
    And the fourth of the Ferment must be.
    If you will have for Red, and White too,
    To Red after this Order you must doe,
    And the White after the same,
    Must be ferment with *Lune* by name,
    And the matter equally divyde
    One for the Red, the other for the White,
    Another like Vessell for the White you must looke,
    As before is taught you in this Booke,
    When your Ferments to your matters be put,
    Then your Vessell close you must shut;
    And sett it to Putrifye as you did before,
    The full tyme as I said of yore :
    And use itt in every degree,
    As in the next Chapter before you may see,
    But looke that you knowe your two Ferments assunder,
    Or elce of your folly itt were great wonder:
    And when from his Blacknesse you have brought itt
White,
    Then have you *Elixir* of wonderfull might:
    Your Red to his perfection is not fully brought,

But your White is perfectly wrought,
Your Red with most strong heate must be fedd
In a close Furnace untill itt be Redd:
When itt is Redd and will melt like waxe,
Then of all that should be nothing laxe,
Now have you a *Stone* of wonderfull might,
Which will take Mercury before his flight,
And command him to stay, and cause him to bring
All Mettalls unto him, and call him their Kinge,
And make such obedyence without Digression,
That of him they shall all take Impression;
Now have you a *Stone* of wonderfull power,
Which conteineth the three Species and the Elements
foure:
Fire in Colour, Water by Effusion,
Earth to sight without delusion,
Aire is in water all men doe knowe,
And thus the foure Elements accordeth nowe:
As for the three Species I will shewe,
How in your *Stone* you may them knowe:
Tincture for Blood perteineth to the Animall,
Moysture the Vegetable part possesse shall;
All Earth is Minerall without any doubt,
Thus keepe we in one Circle and never goe out.
Now have I my *Figure* perfectly wrought,
Yett of the Center I have said right nought.
A Center is a pricke of whatsoever itt be,
Without any manner of divisibilitie;
And made as Nature doth well provide,
So as no Accident may itt divide :
Only by hand but in the Quantitie,
But by noe Element seperate the Qualitie;

If in greate Fire you sett it downe,
A true Salamander itt wilbe found;
If in the Water thou throwe I wis,
It will live there as doth a Fish;
If in the Aire you cast it up hye,
There will it live, and never dye :
If in the Earth thou bury itt fast,
Then will it remaine there, and ever last.
Thus can no Element divide without doubt,
The Center which our Wheele turnes about :
Now how to Multiply your Medicine I trow,
Would doe you much good for to knowe;
For unlesse you know howe to Multiply,
Your Medicine will be spent quickly:
Then would itt put thy minde to much paine,
To thinke that thou must make itt againe:
Therefore the next Chapter shall teach thee right,
To Multiply this *Stone* of wonderfull might.

CHAP. V. HOW TO MULTIPLY.

NOW in this Chapter I meane to shewe,
How to Multiply that thou may knowe:
If Iron to the Load-stone be not put certeinly,
Itt will decreace wonderfully;
The Species of all things both more and lesse each one,
Are mainteyned by reason of Multiplication;
Then if they be not Multiplyed they decay,
But Multiplication makes them be all away.
All things after Conception receive naturall Food,
To mainteine their kind as Nature seeth good:
Soe likewise our *Stone* must needs Multiply,

Or elce the Species of that *Stone* will dye:
And Multiplication must needs be of such thing,
As the thing multiplied takes best likeing.
Fire which burneth perpetually,
If Matter want Fire will dye;
But for to feed our *Stone* rightly,
The way I will shewe presently.
Take your Glasse and Medicine withall,
And in a warme Fire sett itt you shall;
And when itt begins to liquefy,
Put common Mercury to itt by and by;
And itt wilbe devoured anon
By vertue of heate that is in our *Stone*,
And as much as you putt in quantitie,
Soe much doth your Medicine augment truly:
Yett you must have reason not for to cloye,
With overmuch cooling, kind heate thereby:
And as of a Dragme you will make a Pounde,
You may well do itt, if you keep round;
And when it is Multiplied sufficiently,
Then from the Fire set it by.
A man in this Land once I knewe,
That marred that he made, and so may yowe;
Except ye doe as I have taught,
And then neede you to feare nought.
Another I knewe which wanted good direccion,
And at once spent all at one projection.
These knew not howe itt should be multiplyed,
Which things I have taught you at this tyde;
But see that the Mercury wherewith ye Multiply,
Be made soe cleane as itt may be.
Now to make him extend his perfection,

It is needfull to know how to make projeccion:
Whereof in the next Chatper I will treate,
For of Multiplication I will noe more speake.

CHAP. VI. OF PROJECTION.

NOW lacke we but onely this Lesson to take,
Perfectly projection for to make:
Take one parte of the Medicine, and of ☿ ♄ or Tinn,
But see that you make them exceeding cleane;
And when your Mettall doth Liquefy,
Then cast in your parte of Medicine quickly.
Then will it be brought to such a passe,
That all will be as brittle a glass;
Take the brittle substance as it is,
And upon an (100.) To take doe not misse.
That 100. upon 1000. soe still increase you may,
And project noe more when your Tincture doth decay.
This projection is sure without any doubt,
Thus is our Wheele turned round about.
In what Vessell to project I need not to tell,
For a Maister of his Arte knoweth it very well;
To project on Mettalls nowe you knowe,
And to project on mans body nowe will I shewe.
First the Body must be purged well,
And by swetting and bathing be made suttell.
And when you are cleane according to your minde,
Take a dragme of your Medicine with the Quintessence
of Wine;
Such a suddeine alteration itt will showe,
As you need not to feare Corruption noe moe:
Nowe of his Vertues I need not to declare,

They are fully shewne by others elce-where.
Now to the holy Trinitie I thee commend,
Thankeing him my Worke is at an end:
Chargeing thee this Secret from bad men to keepe,
Though with greate Importance of thee they itt seeke;
And beware itt goe not from thy hand,
Except to a perfect honest man.
By Bookes the true Worke I could never finde,
Therefore left I this Booke behinde,
That to whose share soever itt might fall,
By itt they might know our Secretts all.
God grant noe *Multiplyer* meete with my Booke,
Nor noe sinister Clerkes thereon to looke;
Then will they pay their debts surely,
And build Churches, and Steeples very hye;
Keepe itt from these folkes I thee pray,
As thou wilt answere before God att last day:
For whatsoever hath bin said to our worke doth accord,
Therefore give honour, prayse, and thankes to our Lord;
Holy and Reverend be his Name,
Which to me vile Synner hath revealed the same.

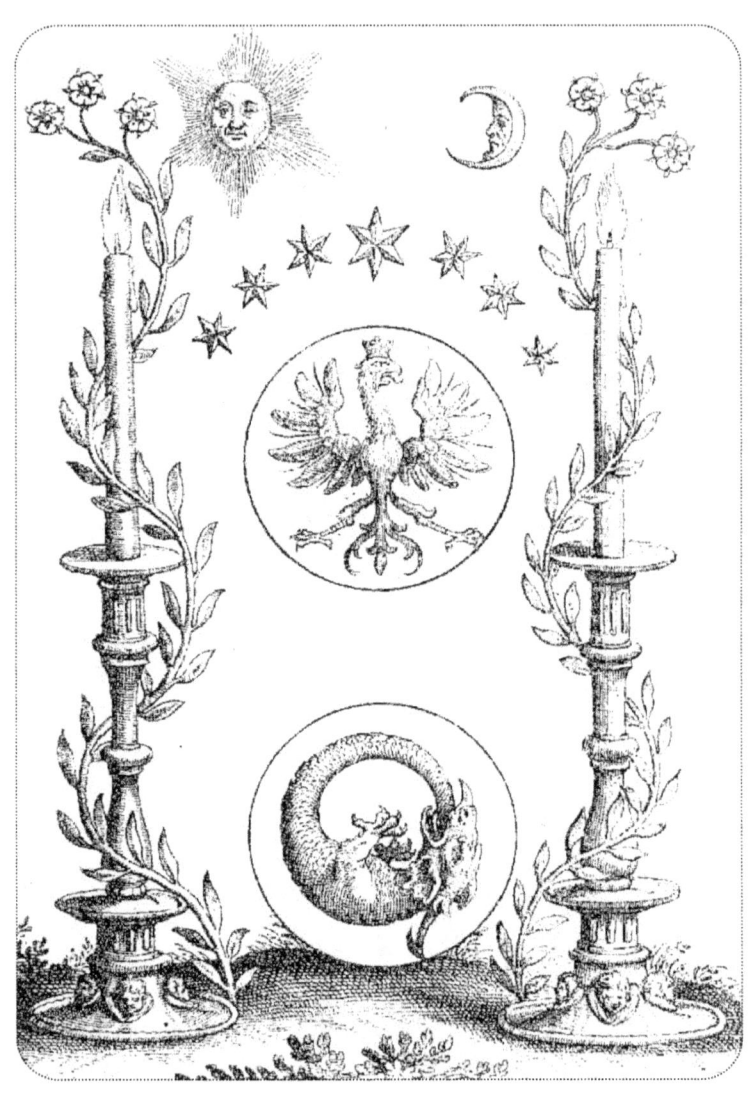

Engravings from J.D. Mylius' *Anatomia Auri,* 1628.

☿

"My son, Horus, embrace the celestial ether, And cleanse your mind from all things material, Lest you sink into the depths of darkness, Into the whirlpool of corporeal matter. Rise, my child, to the heights of heaven, And behold the order of the celestial spheres, The harmony of the stars, and the wisdom of the gods, Which permeates the entire universe.
Revere the Father, the Source of all things, And the Mother, who nourishes all life. Honor the mysteries of the divine powers, And seek the knowledge that transcends all understanding."
—Isis